Praise for

CHICKPEA FLOUR DOES IT ALL

"While Lindsey has deeply explored one of my favorite ingredients (chickpea flour), this book certainly isn't single-note. It's much more than that. Open the cover to discover a robust, creative volume brimming with vibrant, health-supporting seasonal gems. *Chickpea Flour Does It All* is filled with recipes you will want to welcome into your kitchen (and life!) immediately."

—HEIDI SWANSON, author of *Near & Far: Recipes Inspired by Home and Travel*

"Chickpea flour is one of those great secret ingredients—surprisingly versatile, gluten-free, and protein-packed, which makes it perfect for vegan cooking. Lindsey's treasure trove of inventive recipes, beautifully photographed, will inspire cooks of all types to make it a pantry staple."

—TAL RONNEN, chef and author of *Crossroads: Extraordinary Recipes from the Restaurant That Is Reinventing Vegan Cuisine*

"Lindsey S. Love has successfully created an inspiring, useful, and beautiful book using one of the most intriguing ingredients in my pantry: chickpea flour. In this book, you will discover how versatile and delicious this humble flour can be—from Lemony Panelle Sandwich and Spaghetti Squash Fritters to Chickpea Waffle Avocado Toast and Hearty Morning Glory Loaf—I'm excited to try them all!"

—AMY CHAPLIN, chef and James Beard Award–winning cookbook author

"Lindsey's approach makes you fall in love with seasonal, beautiful food that happens to be gluten-free and vegetarian. Her book will encourage you to step out and explore the many uses of chickpea flour through each season."

—ERIN ALDERSON, creator of *Naturally Ella* and author of *The Homemade Flour Cookbook*

THE EXPERIMENT

BECAUSE EVERY BOOK IS A TEST OF NEW IDEAS

"You'll feel good just flipping through this book. *Chickpea Flour Does It All*
is a gorgeous collection of thoughtful recipes that will, of course, get you excited
about the potential of chickpea flour. Lindsey is also masterful at making a life of
seasonally considered wellness feel like it's within anyone's reach."
—LAURA WRIGHT, creator of the *Saveur* award–winning blog *The First Mess*

"*Dolly and Oatmeal* is one of my favorite corners of the internet: bright, friendly,
healthy, and delicious. If you're interested in being a little more mindful of healthy
eating, *Chickpea Flour Does It All* is the book for you! I absolutely cannot wait to try out
the Chickpea Frites, the Alfredo with Watercress and Chives, and the Baked Squash
Tempura. Lindsey's vibrant, inviting photography draws you in and her strong,
knowledgeable voice guides you through the gluten-free world of chickpea flour.
We all could use a little more chickpea flour deliciousness in our lives!"
—STEPHANIE LE, creator of *I Am a Food Blog*

"Yes, chickpea flour really does it all. And it's all because of the
incredible Lindsey S. Love. Her recipes are inspiring, thoughtful,
and most of all, delicious. The new flour power!"
—JESSICA MURNANE, creator of *One Part Plant* and the One Part Podcast

"For years, Lindsey's blog has inspired me with its beautiful photos and fresh
recipes, and she's brought the same recipe wizardry and photo magic to the pages
of *Chickpea Flour Does It All*. I've never seen anything like the Vanilla Bean Lavender
Cupcakes and the Chewy Olive Oil Chocolate Chip Cookies. I cannot wait to make
them and eat them all with less guilt because of how healthy chickpea flour is. Leave
it to Lindsey to get me out the door and on the hunt for chickpea flour in bulk."
—MOLLY YEH, creator of *My Name Is Yeh*

CHICKPEA FLOUR DOES IT ALL

Gluten-Free, Dairy-Free, Vegetarian
Recipes for Every Taste and Season

CHICKPEA FLOUR DOES IT ALL

Gluten-Free, Dairy-Free, Vegetarian
Recipes for Every Taste and Season

LINDSEY S. LOVE

THE EXPERIMENT

NEW YORK

CHICKPEA FLOUR DOES IT ALL: *Gluten-Free, Dairy-Free, Vegetarian Recipes for Every Taste and Season*
Copyright © 2016 by Lindsey S. Love
Photographs © 2016 by Lindsey S. Love

The Experiment, LLC
220 East 23rd Street, Suite 301
New York, NY 10010-4674
www.theexperimentpublishing.com

The Experiment's books are available at special discounts when purchased in bulk for premiums and sales promotions as well as for fund-raising or educational use. For details, contact us at info@theexperimentpublishing.com.

Library of Congress Cataloging-in-Publication Data

Names: Love, Lindsey S., author.
Title: Chickpea flour does it all : Gluten-Free, Dairy-Free, Vegetarian
   Recipes for Every Taste and Season / Lindsey S. Love.
Description: New York : The Experiment, [2016] | Includes index. |
   Description based on print version record and CIP data provided by
   publisher; resource not viewed.
Identifiers: LCCN 2015043928 (print) | LCCN 2015041547 (ebook) | ISBN
   9781615193059 (ebook) | ISBN 9781615193042 (pbk.)
Subjects: LCSH: Gluten-free diet--Recipes. | LCGFT: Cookbooks.
Classification: LCC RM237.86 (print) | LCC RM237.86 .L68 2016 (ebook) | DDC
   641.5/636--dc23
LC record available at http://lccn.loc.gov/2015043928

ISBN 978-1-61519-304-2
Ebook ISBN 978-1-61519-305-9

Cover and text design by Sarah Smith
Cover photographs by Lindsey S. Love
Author photograph by Frank Love

Manufactured in the United States of America
Distributed by Workman Publishing Company, Inc.
Distributed simultaneously in Canada by Thomas Allen & Son Ltd.

First printing April 2016
10 9 8 7 6 5 4 3 2 1

Contents

Introduction

Every weekday morning growing up, my family had a routine so my brother and I wouldn't miss the school bus. We would brush our teeth, shower, get dressed, gather our books into our backpacks, and eat breakfast. He would usually have a muffin or bagel, and me—I would have oatmeal. My mom would always prepare it for me by gently warming milk on the stove, pouring it over instant oats, and topping it off with thinly sliced banana. As I was getting dressed, she would call out "Dolly!" to me when it was ready. Because I still eat oatmeal almost every morning, and because my mom still refers to me as Dolly, *Dolly and Oatmeal* was an obvious choice for my blog's name.

Oatmeal was a large part of my morning routine, but bread and cheese played a very large role in my life growing up in New York as well. As a child with a German/Italian/Jewish/Irish background, I ate my fair share of pasta, bagels, white potatoes, and all sorts of dairy products. For as long as I can remember, though, I had stomach pain, indigestion, and mood swings. It wasn't until I moved out of my parents' house and started cooking for myself that I realized the connection between the food I was eating and the way it made me feel. These issues developed into more pronounced problems, from painful bouts of indigestion to anxiety and even depression.

When my symptoms first started, I was treated by medical doctors who sought to "fix" my difficulties by prescribing medications with side effects that often left me feeling worse than I had previously. From there, I sought to change my diet, and, with the assistance of a homeopathic doctor, I tried a series of plant-based powders, herbs, and natural supplements to detox my system from the medications. After a few months, however, I still did not feel better—my stomach ached, I had gained weight, I was suffering from continued mood swings and anxiety, and it was all beginning to seriously affect important relationships in my life.

While I continued to experiment with changing my diet, I really had no idea where to go or whom to ask for advice. What did it mean to be gluten-free? Should I be vegan? What about eating only raw food? I felt like I was eating healthily, but it still wasn't adding up to feeling any better.

Everywhere I looked, I read confusing and conflicting accounts of what's purported as "good for you." Thanks to some inspiring cookbooks and food blogs, I started to focus on eating whole foods to heal my body from the inside out. I began my diet by including more whole grains, vegetables, and fruits and less take-out, fried food, and snacks. I also started a green smoothie routine in the morning that made me feel like I was doing the right thing—how could eating all that kale and berries be bad? While I began to feel better here and there, I still maintained highs and lows. I knew I wasn't at my best or most vibrant. I always prided myself on being physically fit, playing all kinds of sports, and being active. I recognized that my pursuit for a healthy body and mind was not over.

I finally sought the help of a nutritionist. She started me down a path where I learned the benefits of eating a plant-based, gluten-free, and dairy-free diet, and of being conscious of foods with a high glycemic index that cause a spike in blood sugar, which had often led to irregularity in my mood. Now, I was left feeling light, energized, and, most important, *happy*. The road to healthfulness wasn't the easiest, however—pizza, pasta, sandwiches, and most dairy products were all eliminated from my diet, and I thought my life was basically over. There were so many kitchen mishaps, some minor tantrums, and tons of frustration about where to start. But eventually I became hooked on the new flavors I tasted, the new kitchen experiments I attempted, and the feeling of feeding my mind and body in a better, more thoughtful way. This is what "good for you" is all about!

It was early on in my journey when I was introduced to a flatbread made by mixing chickpea flour, water, olive oil, salt, and pepper and baked in a blazing hot pan. It's known as *farinata* where it originated in Genoa, Italy, or *socca* in Nice, France, where it has been eaten for centuries as well. It became most popular in the 1900s when it was served in Nice as street food accompanied by a glass of chilled rosé. As gluten-free diets have become more popular here in the States, people have begun making this versatile flatbread at home.

I would liken the texture of socca to that of a classic french fry—a warm and crunchy exterior with a smooth and velvety center. My gluten-loving husband, who was my boyfriend at the time, loved it, too, which meant that we could collectively partake in a meal that was both delicious and tolerable for my diet. From then on, chickpea flour would come out weekly when we made socca with our dinner or to accompany soups or stews at lunch. I've included a socca recipe in the July chapter (Everyday Socca, page 115), but socca can be enjoyed any time of year.

As I began developing recipes for freelance projects and for my blog, I experimented with combining chickpea flour and other gluten-free flours and became increasingly confident in the varied texture it offered to many different dishes.

Plus, on its own, chickpea flour can be used in a wide array of recipes for a variety of purposes—in chickpea tofu or savory pancakes, as a thickening agent in soups and sauces, and much more. It's even great in cookies, cakes, and brownies. I then began experimenting with other recipes—a traditional yeast-based gluten-free pizza with crisp asparagus and pea shoots (Chickpea Pizza with Asparagus and Pea Shoot Tangle, page 102); a chickpea fritter sandwich called *panelle* paired with grilled ramps and balsamic vinegar (Lemony Panelle Sandwich with Grilled Ramps and Balsamic Vinegar, page 77); birthday cakes (A Late-Summer Birthday Cake, page 158), blueberry coffee cakes (Lemon-Blueberry Coffee Cake, page 112), and holiday cookies (Jammy Almond Thumbprint Cookies, page 208). I tested them on my husband, who isn't affected by gluten, and realized chickpea flour could be used to make traditional recipes gluten-free. The foods that I thought I had to give up could stay in my diet and still be delicious and nourishing! And with the addition of other flours, like sorghum, oat, and almond, I could enhance the taste and texture of gluten-free baked goods and meals.

So why chickpea flour? While it's still relatively new to many homes here in the United States, chickpea flour can be used to inspire real-life, everyday meals. And chickpea flour has amazing nutritional benefits that stack up against wheat flour and other gluten-free flours as well.

About the Book

Each recipe in this book is gluten-free and dairy-free, vegetarian, and many are vegan as well. As I will expand upon, the recipes are organized by season and month, with ninety-six recipes in all. Of the ninety-six recipes, forty-nine are vegan and are marked with a Ⓥ icon.

The recipes were inspired by my favorite flavors, seasonal ingredients, and beloved dishes, new and old. In some cases, I wanted to re-create a traditional dish—in others I was inspired by the season and the wonderful produce available. In changing my diet to one that is gluten-free, dairy-free, and vegetarian, I didn't lose much. Instead, I gained a wealth of flavors and dishes to try. With some creativity, I was able to embrace the simple pleasure in combining the freshest ingredients to make meals to be shared with friends and family.

In many of the headnotes, I describe how chickpea flour is used in the recipe. You may be surprised by the many ways it can be used: to thicken a soup, as a base for a dressing, in any number of sweet dishes, to make a coating for frying, and in flatbreads and pizza dough. I found that, oftentimes, the best use for chickpea flour in a recipe was an unexpected one.

This book and its recipes are bolstered by a pantry staple that has been around for centuries and is a key ingredient in so many traditional dishes. Chickpea flour helps to create dishes—free of the things that cause discomfort for so many—that everyone can enjoy.

The Facts: What Is Chickpea Flour?

Chickpea flour, also known as garbanzo bean flour, *besan*, or gram flour, is a gluten-free flour—typically ground from raw chickpeas—that's high in protein and also contains healthy unsaturated fat, fiber, vitamins, iron, and magnesium. Unlike some gluten-free flours, chickpea flour is highly nutritious, which leaves you feeling full throughout the day. Chickpea flour contains twenty-three grams of protein in one cup compared to wheat flour's thirteen grams of protein.

Just as wheat flour is a staple in the United States, chickpea flour has been widely produced in countries like India, Nepal, and Pakistan for centuries. In the United States, chickpea flour is quickly gaining attention as a "power flour"—one that is high in nutrients, has a low glycemic index of 27 (anything ranging from 0 to 55 is considered to be a low glycemic index), and makes a great substitute for flours containing gluten. If you were to taste chickpea flour on its own, it has a nutty and bitter taste. When mixed into batters, doughs, slurries, or toasted in a skillet (see page 8), it takes on a smooth flavor and texture that lends itself to sweet and savory recipes alike. In savory recipes this unique flour provides a distinct heartiness; for sweets it creates just the right texture.

When compared to other gluten-free flours, chickpea flour is more affordable, too. A sixteen-ounce package of Bob's Red Mill garbanzo bean flour retails for less than three dollars while the same-size bag of almond flour is five times more expensive.

All-in-all, chickpea flour is versatile, affordable, and healthy. I have found it to be the perfect pantry staple for every day.

CONTAINS (serving size 30 g)	CHICKPEA FLOUR	WHITE RICE FLOUR	WHOLE WHEAT FLOUR
Calories	110	112.5	110
Calories from fat	15	3.75	3.95
Total fat	2 g	.375 g	.393 g
Saturated fat	0 g	0 g	0 g
Trans fat	0 g	0 g	0 g
Cholesterol	0 mg	0 mg	0 mg
Sodium	5 mg	0 mg	0 mg
Total carbohydrates	18 g	24 g	21.3 g
Dietary fiber	5 g	.75 g	3.95 g
Sugars	3 g	0 g	0 g
Protein	6 g	1.5 g	4.73 g
Calcium (%DV)	4 %	0 %	1.6 %
Iron (%DV)	10 %	0 %	6.3 %

My Everyday Kitchen

My pantry is always filled with a rotation of gluten-free whole grains, beans, and legumes. I also have on hand various tree nuts, oils, and vinegars as well as whole-grain, gluten-free flours and nut meals for baking. I find that if I pack my pantry with certain basic foundational items, all I need to do is pick up fresh ingredients when needed to prepare wholesome meals. Everyday cooking in my kitchen is also reliant on the seasonal produce that's available. This approach allows me to be inspired to pick out vibrant produce at the market and prepare it in a thoughtful way. I have included a list of pantry items you will regularly see within this book. Some are better known than others, but all of them can generally be found in major grocery stores nationwide.

HERBS, SPICES, AND SEASONINGS

Throughout this book, I use fine-grain sea salt, unless otherwise specified. I have a large array of ground spices on hand, including cumin, coriander, ginger, nutmeg, allspice, turmeric, and various ground chili peppers, such as chipotle powder, chili powder, and Aleppo pepper. I also stock my spice cabinet with seeds such as caraway, fennel, and cumin that I toast and grind with a mortar and pestle. I try to use fresh herbs as often as possible, so the amount of dried herbs used throughout the book is limited. I usually buy basil, parsley, cilantro, thyme, rosemary, sage, mint, and chives. However, they're not always available fresh in the winter months, so I often keep dried ones handy, and certain hearty herbs like basil, mint, sage, and thyme freeze well.

GLUTEN-FREE FLOURS AND WHOLE GRAINS

Chickpea flour is widely available in stores and is affordable. I use Bob's Red Mill exclusively for the recipes throughout this book. While it is possible to make your own chickpea flour, I do not recommend it to most readers, as it can break or dull your food processor or blender blades, and in some cases may break the machine altogether.

I find that mixing chickpea flour with other flours enhances the flavor and texture of baked goods, cakes, and savory dishes. For scones, I might add sorghum flour to make them more tender. For pancakes, a combination of oat flour and chickpea flour makes for a nuttier flavor. Stone-ground cornmeal is another essential flour I make use of often in breading vegetables and in some baked goods, and I prefer using it over regular cornmeal since its hull and germ are kept in the meal, keeping many of the nutrients intact and giving the flour a coarser texture. In addition, millet flour lends a lovely earthiness to savory baked goods, and brown rice flour can often provide baked goods additional structure without being too dense. I also use raw cacao powder throughout the book because, since it is less processed than cocoa powder, it retains more of its good nutritional qualities. However, if cocoa powder is what you have available to you, you can substitute it at a 1:1 ratio. Lastly, arrowroot powder/flour/ starch comes in handy both for baking and for some savory applications. I use it as a replacement for cornstarch, since it's more easily digestible. Arrowroot is also used as a thickener in many cases, but I love using it in baking too because it acts as a binder while also being quite light.

Cooked quinoa, millet, rolled oats, brown rice, and black rice are all used throughout the book, whether to enhance the texture of a baked good or to add to a hearty stew or salad. Be sure to choose a gluten-free brand of old-fashioned rolled oats. I do try to use local and organic grains when available. Some of these grains take longer than others to cook so I often cook a big batch of one or another kind of grain to have on hand throughout the week. Most of these items are easy to find in your local grocery store or in the bulk section of a natural foods market.

BEANS, LEGUMES, NUTS, AND SEEDS

I use a variety of beans and legumes in my kitchen, including black beans, cannellini beans, English peas, lentils, and peanuts. They offer great texture and flavor in vegetarian dishes, salads, and vegetable stews or as a filler in tacos. Some recipes in this book will call for lentils or two different kinds of mung beans: whole mung beans and split mung beans, also sold as moong dal. A lot of dishes include a variety of tree nuts including almonds, hazelnuts, pine nuts, walnuts, and cashews and seeds such as sunflower seeds, sesame seeds, and pumpkin seeds. You will find that many of the sauce-based recipes throughout the book call for soaked nuts. Generally, nuts soaked for four to five hours are soft enough to blend into a sauce; however, I like to soak them overnight to make them even softer for a smoother, less grainy consistency. Soaked nuts should be drained and rinsed before using. Flaxseed meal and psyllium husk powder are also used intermittently throughout the book for binding purposes where eggs are not being used or for extra binding in baked goods.

PRODUCE AND EGGS

Depending on the season, I keep a variety of produce in my kitchen. In the warmer months I tend to keep more leafy greens, fresh herbs, and summer squash on hand. Early spring is the time for radishes, peppery mustard greens, dandelion greens, herbs, strawberries, and rhubarb. In summer, there is such an array of produce it's hard to keep up, but I tend to go for sour cherries, various summer squashes, cucumbers, sweet corn, tomatoes, berries, and stone fruit.

Colder months are reserved for heartier greens like kale and collard greens. I also keep a variety of winter squash in my kitchen for sweet and savory preparations as well as heartier herbs like sage, thyme, and rosemary. Winter roots are also found in my crisper, ranging from parsnips to turnips to beets.

I tend to spend a little more on local eggs from pasture-raised, hormone-free chickens. The recipes in this book call for pasture-raised eggs. Going to your local farmers' market and speaking with the growers is a wonderful opportunity to connect with where your food comes from as well as the farmers who supply it—I talk to the farmers and hear their stories. It's great to learn why the hens laid different-colored eggs, how long a farm has been in operation, or even to see how long the eggs will keep in your refrigerator. I've accumulated a wealth of knowledge, from how to store herbs and leafy greens to where the best spot in your refrigerator is to keep summer berries.

FATS

Many dishes in this book rely upon healthy fats, including extra virgin olive oil, unrefined extra virgin coconut oil, and sunflower oil. Each lends its own taste to given dishes, some adding earthiness, others moisture and/or flavor. I generally use olive oil for savory dishes, but in some cases it's utilized in baked goods like cakes (see Chocolate Olive Oil Cakes, page 42) and cookies (see Chewy Olive Oil Chocolate Chip Cookies, page 156). I use sunflower oil for frying because it's a great high-heat oil that doesn't burn or smoke. Coconut oil is mostly reserved for sweet baked goods, and, on occasion, I sauté vegetables with it to give them added flavor.

VINEGARS, LEMON JUICE, TAMARI, AND MISO

You'll find I use different vinegars throughout the book to bring a certain flavor to a dish. An aged balsamic vinegar is great to have on hand for cooking, lending its own distinct flavor to a meal. Red wine vinegar is mostly used for salad dressings, while I generally use apple cider vinegar for making vegan buttermilk in baked goods like Baked Buttermilk Onion Rings (see page 172) and Buttermilk Chickpea Corn Bread (see page 184). Rice vinegar is mostly reserved for Asian-inspired dishes, giving sauces a lovely punch. Whenever lemon juice is called for I prefer to use fresh. Bottled lemon juice may contain preservatives, added sugar, or water. Not all miso is gluten-free so be sure to choose a gluten-free brand. I really enjoy the flavor of buckwheat- or chickpea-based miso pastes. As for tamari, I prefer using a low-sodium variety, and, while it is generally gluten-free, always check the brand you use to make sure it doesn't contain any wheat.

SWEETENERS

I use various sweeteners to cultivate a specific taste, to keep the glycemic index low, or to add more or less liquid in a recipe. The sweetener used most often in this book is coconut sugar. It derives from coconut trees and has a very low glycemic index, reducing the rate of spike in blood sugar after eating. I enjoy using this sweetener in most baked goods, including muffins, cookies, and cakes. Organic grade B maple syrup is another sweetener utilized frequently throughout the book. While it does have a higher glycemic index than coconut sugar, when used sparingly it lends a unique flavor to any dish. I use raw honey and muscovado sugar as well, and unrefined organic cane sugar modestly. I also use pure vanilla extract and vanilla beans to flavor baked goods.

Throughout the book I call for full-fat coconut milk. I prefer using 13.5-ounce cans of Thai Kitchen Organic Coconut Milk, as I find that it gives me the best flavor and results in baking and savory preparations. The other milk I call for is unsweetened almond milk. I call for unsweetened because many nondairy milks can be loaded with some sort of sweetener. Starting with the most basic and unflavored ingredients is important for achieving the best flavors.

OTHER

Like many other ingredients that I've outlined, I tend to purchase store-bought items in their most basic state. For instance, I buy unsweetened organic applesauce and vegetable broth for soups and stews, as I prefer to add sweetness and salt myself depending on what I'm preparing. Because I often bake with nut butters like almond butter, I purchase it with no salt added. Instant or fast-rising yeast is my go-to for bread making or pizza dough, and I always make sure that I'm buying aluminum-free and gluten-free baking powder (some brands of baking powder can include wheat starch, which contains gluten). I generally buy pantry items like harissa paste and tahini paste at specialty stores; however, they can also be readily found in many grocery stores.

Toasting Chickpea Flour

Toasting chickpea flour is a great way to add a ton of flavor to a dish. I love adding toasted chickpea flour to soups (see Sunchoke and Leek Soup, page 20; Spring Onion and Lemongrass Stew with Cauliflower and Yams, page 73; and Sweet Corn and Cilantro Chowder, page 135); while it does act as a thickener, toasted chickpea flour also adds a subtle nutty taste, which provides an additional depth of flavor. It's also great in vegetable burgers, patties, and fritters (Breakfast Sweet Potato Cakes and Baby Arugula Bowl, page 15; Beetballs with Rosemary White Bean Cream, page 178; Spaghetti Squash Fritters, page 176; Moroccan-Spiced Lentil and Pumpkin Burgers, page 191; and Celery Root Latkes, page 203), where it is used as a binder and dry ingredient; plus it provides a lovely and unique flavor you can't get from any other flour.

Place 1 cup of chickpea flour in a large skillet, turn the heat to medium, and stir. Keep stirring for five to seven minutes, until the flour is lightly browned and has a nutty fragrance. Place in a bowl or on a plate and let it cool at room temperature. Store toasted chickpea flour in an airtight container at room temperature if not using right away.

Thoughts on Seasonality

I structured this book with recipes grouped by month to highlight the fruits and vegetables that are fresh and seasonal at each respective time of year. Since some produce may vary regionally, use the recipes as inspiration depending on what is seasonally available in your area. Part of the fun in cooking is taking inspiration from recipes, adding what you like or what's available to you, and making a delicious meal out of it. While the recipes are specific in terms of amounts and quantities, you can often take the base of a winter recipe and instead incorporate summer produce. Or prepare a spring polenta dish in winter with roasted root vegetables.

Some of my recipes call for fruits and vegetables found at the grocery store that may not be available locally in your area, like bananas or kiwi. Be sure to try to buy organic options whenever possible. Also, keep in mind the Environmental Working Group's "Dirty Dozen," a list of the fruits and vegetables with the most pesticides. The produce on that list should definitely be purchased from organic growers. If you're buying from your local farmers' market, some small farmers (even if they aren't certified organic) do not use pesticides. The "Clean Fifteen" can be purchased from conventionally grown sources when organic options aren't accessible to you.

Eating seasonally to me is not only about eating what produce is available but also being conscious of the ebbs and flows of what we are seeking to nourish ourselves. In winter, I crave chocolate; it's nourishing to me and provides comfort in those cold brutal months. In spring, I feel a natural urge to eat outside, breathe fresh air, and eat more salads. I hope you can take inspiration from the monthly meals I have created and think of chickpea flour as a year-round pantry staple.

Winter Months

Winter is the season when we feel
that deep inclination to sleep
longer, go to bed earlier, and,
perhaps, not leave the house on
a given weekend. But it's also
the time when we get to enjoy
winter root vegetables; the tart,
juicy flavors of fresh citrus fruits;
nourishing soups; and heartier fare
in general. I created the recipes
in the winter months' section to
use much of the produce we see
at the market or grocery store at
this time, but I also gave a nod to
the natural inclinations of how we
generally eat in the winter. Long
gone are the days when a cold,
crisp salad is a preference; it's the
time when we don't mind stewing
a pot of vegetables for a couple
of hours if it means warmth and
nourishment. Here are crackers,
a flavorful flatbread, an out-of-
this-world chocolate banana loaf,
and a personal favorite: a chickpea
banh mi. I endeavored to make the
recipes flavorful, fun, and vibrant
to keep your spirits high during
winter's pause.

Sautéed Pear and Sage Pancakes with Almonds

MAKES: 8 TO 10 PANCAKES // **SERVES:** 4 // **PREP TIME:** 10 MINUTES // **COOK TIME:** 30 MINUTES

Gluten-free pancakes were something that eluded my kitchen for quite some time after I went gluten-free. The batter was always too runny, and the pancakes never held together long enough to be flipped over. Then, I read an article that simply said to increase the amount of flour to reach a consistency that was thicker, and I've never looked back. These pancakes are slightly sweet and hearty without being dense, hold together perfectly, and are just as delicious when eaten as leftovers. Sautéing the pear slices is a really quick and tasty way to soften and warm them, and the sage is great for making this morning meal not too sweet. While the pears may be sweet enough for some, I really like drizzling these pancakes with warmed maple syrup.

¾ cup (90 g) chickpea flour

¾ cup (85 g) oat flour

1 tablespoon cane sugar

1 teaspoon ground cinnamon

½ teaspoon baking powder

¼ teaspoon baking soda

¼ teaspoon sea salt

1 large egg

1 cup (240 ml) almond milk

2 tablespoons extra virgin olive oil

½ teaspoon pure vanilla extract

1 tablespoon plus 1 teaspoon coconut oil

1 firm but ripe pear, cored and sliced thin

1½ teaspoons minced sage, plus extra for garnish

¼ cup (35 g) toasted almonds, roughly chopped

Maple syrup

❶ Preheat oven to 200°F (95°C) and line a baking sheet with foil; set aside.

❷ In a large mixing bowl, combine the flours, sugar, cinnamon, baking powder, baking soda, and salt. In a separate bowl, whisk together the egg, milk, olive oil, and vanilla. Gently pour the wet ingredients into the dry, mixing thoroughly to combine.

❸ Heat a large skillet over medium heat; add 2 teaspoons coconut oil; once melted, add 2 tablespoons of batter for each pancake. Cook 2 to 3 minutes on each side; place the cooked pancakes on the baking sheet and place in the oven to keep warm. Repeat with the remaining batter, adding more coconut oil to the skillet as needed.

❹ While the pancakes are keeping warm, heat the same skillet over medium heat. Melt the remaining 2 teaspoons of coconut oil; add the pear slices (reserving some slices for garnish) and cook, stirring occasionally, until lightly browned, 4 to 5 minutes. In the last 30 seconds, add the minced sage and cook until wilted and fragrant.

❺ Plate pancakes; top with a few pear slices, sage, almonds, and syrup.

Breakfast Sweet Potato Cakes
and Baby Arugula Bowl Ⓥ

MAKES: 8 TO 10 CAKES // **SERVES:** 4 TO 5 // **PREP TIME:** 3 HOURS // **COOK TIME:** 40 MINUTES

This sweet potato bowl is definitely a departure from a traditional breakfast bowl, but there are some mornings where we all crave something savory that isn't an egg dish. The potato-cake mix can be made the day before and refrigerated so that the only task left is to cook them on the stove. I really like making the patties in advance, refrigerating or freezing them, and putting a breakfast bowl together without having to worry about not having enough time.

SWEET POTATO CAKES

2 medium-large sweet potatoes (about 600 g)

2 tablespoons plus 2 teaspoons extra virgin olive oil

½ red onion, finely diced

1 garlic clove, minced

1 large egg, whisked

2 tablespoons chopped chives

½ teaspoon ground cumin

½ teaspoon sea salt

Pinch of ground nutmeg

½ cup (60 g) chickpea flour, toasted

ARUGULA BOWL

1 small shallot, minced

2 teaspoons champagne vinegar

1 teaspoon Dijon mustard

Sea salt and freshly ground pepper

3 tablespoons extra virgin olive oil

¼ teaspoon maple syrup

4 cups (80 g) baby arugula

1 ripe avocado, cubed

¼ cup toasted sesame seeds

❶ Preheat oven to 400°F (200°C) and line a rimmed baking sheet with parchment paper. Set aside. Prick the potatoes all over with a fork and place on the baking sheet. Bake for 1 hour, until a sharp knife can easily pierce the flesh; set potatoes aside until cool enough to handle.

❷ While the potatoes are cooling, heat 2 teaspoons of oil in a skillet over medium heat. Once hot, add the onion and cook for 2 minutes, until soft; add the garlic and cook 30 seconds more. Remove from the heat and set aside.

❸ Use a spoon to scoop the cooled potato flesh from the skin and place it in a large bowl. Then mash the potatoes with a fork or potato masher until smooth and add the sautéed onions and garlic.

❹ Add the egg, chives, cumin, salt, and nutmeg; fold the mixture until thoroughly incorporated. In three portions, add the toasted chickpea flour, incorporating it entirely each time. Let the mixture rest in the refrigerator for at least 3 hours or overnight. If the mixture is overly wet and sticky, add more flour, 1 tablespoon at a time, until easy to handle.

❺ Heat 2 tablespoons of oil in a skillet over medium heat. Pinch off a scant 2 tablespoons of the mixture, roll it into a ball, and then flatten to about ¾ an inch. Once the oil is hot and shimmering, cook the patties in batches, taking care not to overcrowd the pan.

❻ Cook for 3 to 4 minutes on each side, until lightly browned and crisp. Place on a paper towel–lined plate to soak up any extra oil. Repeat with remaining patties, adding more oil as needed.

❼ To make the dressing, in a small mixing bowl combine the shallot and vinegar. Let sit for a few minutes to soften; then add the mustard, and salt and pepper, to taste. Whisk in oil and maple syrup until emulsified; set dressing aside.

❽ In a large bowl, toss together the arugula, avocado, and dressing.

❾ Divide the arugula among four to five bowls and place warm sweet potato cakes on top; garnish with the toasted sesame seeds.

Onion Poppy Seed Bread

MAKES: ONE 8 X 4-INCH LOAF // **SERVES:** 6 TO 8 // **PREP TIME:** 45 MINUTES TO 1 HOUR
COOK TIME: 45 TO 50 MINUTES

This is an easy bread that comes together quite simply. I enjoy making this on a Saturday or Sunday so I can have fresh bread throughout the week to eat with morning eggs, for an avocado toast snack, or to serve with a stew or soup. The combination of onions and poppy seeds is subtle, but when toasted, the flavors really come through.

If you don't care for onions or poppy seeds, simply take them out, or replace them with flavors to your liking. The consistency of the prebaked dough should be like thick cookie dough, however, not like cookie dough that you form into balls. It should be fluid and spread easily with a spatula or wooden spoon. When the bread is baked, it will be about 3 inches in height with a subtle density while also being light.

1 cup (140 g) brown rice flour

1 cup (120 g) chickpea flour

½ cup (55 g) sorghum flour

½ cup (60 g) arrowroot powder

1 tablespoon poppy seeds

1 packet (roughly 2½ teaspoons) instant yeast

2 teaspoons psyllium husk powder

2 teaspoons sea salt

2 large eggs

½ cup (75 g) finely diced onion

¼ cup (60 ml) extra virgin olive oil

2 tablespoons honey

¾ cup (180 ml) water

1 Use your fingers to lightly grease an 8 x 4-inch loaf pan with olive oil and line with a piece of parchment paper with wings that overhang on two sides. Turn oven to 200°F (90°C); when the oven reaches temperature turn it off.

2 Whisk together the flours, arrowroot, seeds, yeast, psyllium husk, and salt in a mixer bowl. Attach the dough hook to an electric mixer; with the setting on medium, add the eggs, onion, oil, and honey and mix until the mixture is wet and crumbly, scraping down the sides as you go. With the mixer still on medium, drizzle the water in a little bit at a time, until the mixture resembles a thick batter (the batter should be thick but fluid enough to spread into the pan easily).

3 Gently transfer the dough to the prepared loaf pan; use a rubber spatula to even out the surface. Lightly grease a piece of plastic wrap with your fingers and loosely cover the top of the pan. Place in the warmed oven for 30 to 45 minutes, until dough has risen up to meet the plastic wrap. Remove from the oven and set aside.

4 Heat oven to 350°F (180°C). Bake in the center of your oven for 45 to 50 minutes, until golden brown. When the surface of the bread is tapped, it should sound hollow.

5 Allow the loaf to cool completely before slicing. Bread is best stored in the refrigerator, or can be frozen for up to 1 month.

Za'atar Crackers Ⓥ

MAKES: 50 TO 60 CRACKERS // SERVES: 4 TO 6 // PREP TIME: 35 MINUTES
COOK TIME: 18 TO 20 MINUTES

Za'atar is a really lovely Middle Eastern spice blend that is generally made with dried herbs, sesame seeds, sumac, and salt. It can be used for seasoning meats, stirred into hummus and other dips, or used as a flavoring for roasted vegetables. Many grocery stores carry za'atar in the spice aisle; however, I provide a small-batch recipe here that can easily be doubled or tripled, since za'atar can be stored for months in a lidded jar in the cabinet. The crackers are great to make as a snack or appetizer served with hummus or your favorite dip. I generally make the crackers a day in advance if I know I'm going to have company over, or for snacks throughout the week.

ZA'ATAR SPICE

2 tablespoons dried oregano

2 tablespoons dried thyme

1 tablespoon toasted sesame seeds

1 teaspoon sumac

¼ teaspoon sea salt

CRACKERS

2 cups (240 g) chickpea flour, plus more for dusting

1 teaspoon baking powder

½ teaspoon sea salt

2 tablespoons coconut milk

2 tablespoons extra virgin olive oil, plus more for brushing

3 to 4 tablespoons water

2 to 3 tablespoons za'atar

Large-grain sea salt

❶ To make the za'atar spice blend, crush the oregano and thyme with a mortar and pestle; stir in the seeds, sumac, and salt. Transfer to a lidded jar (can be stored at room temperature for up to 6 months).

❷ Preheat oven to 350°F (180°C) and line two baking sheets with parchment paper; set aside.

❸ In a large bowl, whisk together the flour, baking powder, and salt. Add the milk and oil; use your fingers to evenly distribute, until clumpy. Add the water a little bit at a time, incorporating with your hands. Once dough comes together, knead for a few minutes, until smooth. If the dough feels dry and is cracking, knead in more water, a teaspoon at a time, until smooth. Cover with a damp towel, and let rest for 10 minutes.

❹ Place a large piece of parchment on a flat work surface and sprinkle with flour; divide the dough into two equal pieces. Place one piece on the work surface and sprinkle with flour; flatten the dough with your palm and roll out into a large rectangle with ⅛-inch thickness. Using a sharp knife, cut into large 3-inch rectangles, and transfer to a baking sheet. Using a pastry brush, lightly brush the tops of the crackers with oil, then gently press the za'atar blend into the tops of the crackers and sprinkle with large-grain salt. Bake for 18 to 20 minutes, rotating halfway through, until lightly browned. Remove and let cool completely before serving.

❺ Crackers can be stored in an airtight container at room temperature for 1 week.

Sunchoke and Leek Soup ⓥ

MAKES: 4 CUPS // **SERVES:** 4 // **PREP TIME:** 10 MINUTES // **COOK TIME:** 30 TO 35 MINUTES

Sunchokes, or Jerusalem artichokes, are the roots or tubers of a flower related to sunflowers, and although they share part of their name with artichokes, they are not related to them. Sunchokes have a sweet, nutty flavor and are similar in appearance to ginger root. They are great for roasting, for purees, and for soups. But because they lack a lot of starch, many sunchoke soups are made with potatoes to thicken them up. However, chickpea flour is a great way of adding texture and, when it's toasted, a really great flavor. As the soup cools, it will thicken quite a bit. If it's stored in the refrigerator, the soup will become stiff but will resume its fluid consistency when heated and whisked.

½ cup (60 g) chickpea flour

1 tablespoon coconut oil

1 tablespoon extra virgin olive oil

2 leeks, rinsed and white and light green parts diced

2 garlic cloves, chopped

2 teaspoons fresh thyme (or 1 teaspoon dried thyme), plus more for garnish

1 pound (450 g) sunchokes, peeled and cubed

4 cups (960 ml) water

1 bay leaf

1½ teaspoons sea salt, plus more to taste

1 tablespoon lemon juice

Sunflower microgreens, for serving

Freshly ground pepper

❶ Place the flour in a skillet over medium heat and stir with a wooden spoon for 6 to 7 minutes, until lightly browned and fragrant. Remove the flour from the skillet and place in a bowl to cool.

❷ Heat the coconut oil and olive oil in a large soup pot over medium heat. Add the leeks and cook until soft, about 5 minutes; add the garlic and thyme; cook for another 30 to 40 seconds, until fragrant. Add the sunchokes, water, bay leaf, and salt; turn the heat to high and bring to a boil. Turn the heat down and bring to a simmer, cover, and cook for 20 minutes, until sunchokes are fork-tender.

❸ Whisk in the chickpea flour and return the heat to high and bring to a boil, until soup has thickened, about 3 minutes. In batches, puree the soup in a high-speed blender or food processor, until silky and smooth. Transfer the pureed soup back to the pot and stir in the lemon juice; taste and adjust the salt, if needed. Ladle into soup bowls and top with sunflower microgreens, thyme, and ground pepper.

Ginger-Shiitake Miso Broth
with Chickpea Tofu ⓥ

SERVES: 4 AS A SIDE OR APPETIZER // **PREP TIME:** 4 TO 12 HOURS // **COOK TIME:** 30 TO 35 MINUTES

Many traditional tofu products contain genetically modified soy and have little to no nutritional integrity. This chickpea variation on the long-established soy tofu is a wonderful way to make homemade tofu while retaining many nutritional properties. The broth is revitalizing and light, but also provides subtle heat from the ginger. This soup is great to serve on a cold, snowy day when all you want to feel is warmth in your body.

CHICKPEA TOFU

2 cups (480 ml) water

1 cup (120 g) chickpea flour

½ teaspoon sea salt

BROTH

5 cups (1,200 ml) water

1 ounce (28 g) dried shiitake mushrooms, stemmed

One 1-inch piece of ginger, sliced into ¼-inch pieces

3 to 4 tablespoons gluten-free mellow white miso

¼ cup (28 g) chopped scallions

Half dozen bok choy leaves, chopped

Red pepper flakes (optional)

❶ Lightly grease an 8 x 8-inch pan and set aside.

❷ In a saucepan, whisk together the water, flour, and salt. Turn the heat to medium and continue whisking for about 5 to 6 minutes. Place the whisk aside and continue stirring with a rubber spatula until the mixture is thick and pulls away from the sides of the pan, about 10 to 12 minutes.

❸ Quickly pour the mixture into the baking pan and use your spatula to spread evenly into the sides and corners of pan. Let cool at room temperature; once cool, place in the refrigerator for at least 4 hours or overnight.

❹ Remove from the refrigerator and invert onto a large cutting board. Slice into ½-inch chunks and store in a lidded container in the refrigerator.

❺ To make the broth, bring the water, mushrooms, and ginger to a boil over high heat. Cover the pot, reduce the heat to low, and simmer for 30 minutes. Use a slotted spoon to remove the ginger and mushrooms. (Alternatively, you can keep the mushrooms in the soup.)

❻ In a small bowl, whisk 3 tablespoons of miso paste with ¼ cup of the broth; add back into the pot, stir, and taste; add an additional tablespoon of miso if the broth needs it, and turn the heat to low. Stir in the scallions and bok choy, and cook for an additional 2 to 3 minutes, until bok choy is wilted.

❼ Divide the soup and tofu among four bowls; serve with a pinch of red pepper flakes, if desired.

Caraway Spätzle with Kale and Balsamic Onions

SERVES: 4 // **PREP TIME:** 1 HOUR 10 MINUTES // **COOK TIME:** 35 MINUTES

I first tasted spätzle when I visited a friend's family in Salzburg, Austria, as a teenager. I can remember being put off by its foreign name, not knowing exactly what it was that I ordered. But when the waiter served me my meal, I was pleasantly surprised to find that it was an almost pasta-like dish without the red sauce, served with cheese and herbs. As I found out later on, spätzle is served in a few European countries and some Eastern European countries that all have different ways of preparing the dish with various sauces and additions. Spätzle is quite simple to make. Many recipes call for a spätzle maker; however, spätzle can be made by using a slotted spoon or a colander. The batter can be prepared ahead of time, and the spätzle noodles take barely 1 minute to cook. I really enjoy the subtlety of the crushed caraway seeds here, which I urge you to try, but if you're opposed to that flavor, it can be replaced with ground nutmeg.

½ teaspoon caraway seeds

1 cup (120 g) chickpea flour

½ teaspoon sea salt, plus more to taste

2 large eggs

¼ cup (60 ml) water

1 tablespoon extra virgin olive oil

1 medium onion, sliced thin

1 tablespoon balsamic vinegar

Freshly ground pepper

1 cup (130 g) chopped kale

¼ cup (15 g) chopped parsley

❶ Toast the caraway seeds in a small skillet over medium-low heat, shaking the pan every few seconds to avoid scorching. Continue toasting seeds for 2 to 3 minutes, until lightly browned and fragrant. Remove from the heat and let cool. Crush the seeds with a mortar and pestle until finely ground.

❷ In a large bowl, mix together the ground caraway, flour, and salt. Make a well in the center; add the eggs and water; using a wooden spoon, slowly mix and incorporate the ingredients until a smooth dough forms—it should look like pancake batter. Cover with plastic wrap and refrigerate for at least 1 hour or overnight.

❸ Fill a large pot three-quarters of the way with water and bring to a boil; set a colander in the sink. Place another colander over the top of the pot or use a slotted spoon, and push the dough through the holes with a rubber spatula into the boiling water. (If using a slotted spoon you will do this in batches.) Spätzle will float to the surface quickly; once it does, use a slotted spoon or sieve to transfer to the colander in the sink; rinse with cold water to stop them from cooking. Set aside.

❹ Heat the oil in a large skillet over medium heat; once the oil is hot and shimmering, add the onion and stir. Cook for 15 minutes, stirring every few minutes to prevent burning. When the onions are lightly browned and caramelized in places, add the balsamic vinegar, and salt and pepper, to taste; cook until liquid is reduced to half, about 1 minute. Add the kale and sauté until wilted, about 1 to 2 minutes. Add the spätzle to the pan and cook for 5 minutes, until heated through and hot.

❺ Remove from the heat and mix in the parsley and more pepper, to taste.

Chocolate Banana Loaf

MAKES: ONE 9 X 5-INCH LOAF // **SERVES:** 8 TO 10 // **PREP TIME:** 15 MINUTES
COOK TIME: 45 TO 50 MINUTES

Banana bread was perhaps the first thing I remember baking with my mother when I was a child. I specifically remember the two kitchen-stained index cards with recipes for banana bread and applesauce bread. That banana bread recipe was made at least two to three times per year, for special occasions, long weekends, or just to have the scent of banana bread waft through the house. This iteration of banana bread is a mildly more decadent one. More of a dessert loaf than a breakfast loaf, this bread is moist and rich with nuggets of chopped chocolate throughout. I indicate to use bittersweet chocolate, preferably between 60 percent to 70 percent cacao; chocolate that has less than 60 percent cacao will likely prove too sweet for this loaf, and chocolate with more than 70 percent cacao is too bitter.

¾ cup (90 g) chickpea flour

½ cup (50 g) almond flour

½ cup (57 g) oat flour

¼ cup (20 g) cacao powder

1 teaspoon baking powder

½ teaspoon baking soda

½ teaspoon sea salt

2 large eggs

½ cup (72 g) coconut sugar

1½ cups (180 ml) banana puree
(from 3 to 4 very ripe bananas)

½ cup (120 ml) sunflower oil

1 teaspoon pure vanilla extract

½ cup (65 g) chopped bittersweet
chocolate (60 to 70 percent cacao)

❶ Preheat oven to 350°F (180°C), grease a 9 x 5-inch loaf pan, and line with parchment paper, letting the paper hang over the sides.

❷ In a large mixing bowl, whisk together the flours, cacao powder, baking powder, baking soda, and salt; set aside. In another large bowl, whisk together the eggs and sugar until combined; add the banana puree, oil, and vanilla; whisk until mixed. Use a spatula to mix the dry ingredients into the wet a little at a time, until completely incorporated. Fold in the chopped chocolate, reserving a handful for topping the loaf.

❸ Transfer the batter to the prepared loaf pan; use a spatula to smooth out the surface; sprinkle with remaining chopped chocolate.

❹ Bake in the center of the oven for 45 to 50 minutes, until a cake tester comes out clean and the loaf is lightly browned and pulling away from the pan. Transfer the pan to a rack; allow loaf to cool for 20 minutes. Use parchment overhang to remove the loaf from the pan, let the loaf cool completely before slicing.

❺ Loaf can be stored in an airtight container at room temperature for 3 to 4 days.

Collard Wrap with Turmeric Scramble ⓥ

SERVES: 2 TO 4 // **PREP TIME:** 10 MINUTES // **COOK TIME:** 15 MINUTES

Chickpea flour can be an awesome substitute for egg-like breakfast scrambles. It's tasty, nutritious, and the flavors added can vary. To make a scramble, you start with a simple batter that incorporates flour, water, salt, pepper, and whatever spices, herbs, or greens you prefer. It's also a perfect addition to a breakfast wrap. While a tortilla wrap is equally as delicious, when I want to incorporate some greens in my morning meal, I go the route of a collard wrap. The greens are steamed ever so slightly to make them more malleable, while also retaining a bit of crunch.

1 cup (120 g) chickpea flour

½ teaspoon sea salt,
plus more to taste

¼ teaspoon ground turmeric

Freshly ground pepper

1 cup (240 ml) water

2 tablespoons extra virgin olive oil

1 shallot, minced

1 garlic clove, minced

2 tablespoons chopped cilantro

4 collard green leaves

1 ripe avocado, pitted

2 teaspoons lemon juice

½ teaspoon ground cumin

Sprouts or microgreens

❶ In a bowl, whisk together the flour, salt, turmeric, and pepper, to taste; add the water; whisk until smooth and no lumps remain. Set aside.

❷ Heat the oil in an 8- to 10-inch skillet over medium heat; add the shallot and cook for 1 to 2 minutes, until soft and translucent. Add the garlic and cook for another 30 to 40 seconds, until fragrant.

❸ Add the chickpea batter and allow it to cook undisturbed for 4 to 5 minutes, until sides are bubbly; flip over and cook for another minute, then add the cilantro and use a spatula to break the mix up into a scramble. Cook for 1 to 2 minutes more, until the batter is completely cooked through. Remove from the heat and set aside.

❹ Slice the thick stalk from the bottoms of the collard greens; turn the collard green over to the backside and use a paring knife to shave the stem so it's flush with the leaf—this makes rolling and chewing easier.

❺ Bring a small pot of water to a boil; one at a time, steam the collard leaves for about 10 seconds, until bright green and a bit soft; use a paper towel to dab any moisture and repeat with remaining leaves.

❻ Mash the avocado with the lemon juice, cumin, and salt to taste, and set aside. Lay the leaves horizontally and spread each with the avocado mash, leaving about a 1-inch border along the sides; top with the scramble and a handful of sprouts or microgreens. Take the bottom of the wrap and fold it over the filling, tuck in the sides, and continue rolling and tucking until you get to the top. With the seam on the bottom, slice the wraps in half and secure with a toothpick, if needed.

Hearty Morning Glory Loaf

MAKES: ONE 9 X 5-INCH LOAF // **SERVES:** 8 TO 10 // **PREP TIME:** 25 MINUTES

COOK TIME: 60 TO 70 MINUTES

The first time I ever had a morning glory muffin was from Morning Glory Farm on Martha's Vineyard, Massachusetts. They are well-known for their fresh-baked muffins, scones, pies, and cakes. But I remember that muffin quite vividly: moist, slightly sweet with flecks of tender apple, warm spices, and ribbons of carrot. This recipe is reminiscent of that muffin I had on Morning Glory Farm—earthy but sweet, and hearty but tender. I prefer to use Honeycrisp apples here, but if they're not available to you, Gala, Pink Lady, and Fuji apples make great replacements.

⅔ cup (96 g) coconut sugar

½ cup (120 ml) sunflower oil

2 large eggs

½ cup (75 g) applesauce

1 teaspoon pure vanilla extract

1 cup (120 g) chickpea flour

½ cup (70 g) brown rice flour

¼ cup (30 g) arrowroot powder

1 teaspoon baking powder

1 teaspoon baking soda

1 teaspoon freshly grated nutmeg

1 teaspoon psyllium husk powder

½ teaspoon sea salt

Zest from 1 orange

1 apple, peeled and finely diced (Honeycrisp preferred)

1 cup (100 g) grated carrots

½ cup (50 g) raw walnuts, chopped

¼ cup (18 g) coconut flakes

1 tablespoon gluten-free old-fashioned rolled oats

2 teaspoons poppy seeds

❶ Preheat oven to 350°F (180°C), grease a 9 x 5-inch loaf pan, and line with parchment paper, leaving enough to overhang on two sides; set aside.

❷ In a large mixing bowl, whisk together the sugar, oil, eggs, applesauce, and vanilla. In another large bowl, whisk together the flours, arrowroot, baking powder, baking soda, nutmeg, psyllium husk, salt, and zest. Add the wet ingredients to the dry and fold in the apple, carrots, walnuts, and coconut.

❸ Transfer the batter to the prepared loaf pan. Top with oats and poppy seeds and bake for 60 to 70 minutes, rotating halfway through for even baking, until a cake tester inserted into the center comes out clean.

❹ Remove from the oven and place on a rack to cool. Remove the loaf from the pan after 20 minutes and allow to cool completely before slicing.

Chickpea Waffle Avocado Toast

MAKES: EIGHTEEN 4-INCH WAFFLES // **SERVES:** 6 TO 8 // **PREP TIME:** 10 MINUTES
COOK TIME: 25 MINUTES

I'm pretty sure that as soon as avocado toast hit the airwaves no one looked at toast the same. There are so many different avocado toast combinations that continue to keep toast relevant and delicious. This variation is an absolute favorite of mine and something that is continually on repeat for weekend breakfasts. The waffles are made savory and in a smaller size to emulate a slice of toast; however, if you prefer you can make larger waffles by using more batter—just be sure to adjust the cook time, as it may take longer to cook the larger waffles.

2 cups (240 g) chickpea flour

1½ teaspoons baking powder

1½ teaspoons sea salt,
plus more to taste

¼ teaspoon freshly ground pepper,
plus more to taste

2 large eggs

1¼ cups (300 ml) almond milk

⅓ cup (80 ml) extra virgin olive oil

1 tablespoon chopped chives,
plus more for garnish

2 to 3 ripe avocados, sliced

1 lemon

¼ cup (35 g) hemp seeds

❶ In a large bowl, whisk together the flour, baking powder, salt, and pepper. In a separate bowl, whisk the eggs, milk, oil, and chives. Add the wet mix to the dry mix and combine thoroughly.

❷ Heat waffle maker on medium-high. Heat oven to 200°F (95°C) and place a baking sheet lined with parchment paper inside.

❸ Spoon roughly 2 tablespoons worth of batter onto the waffle iron; cook about 1½ minutes, until edges are golden and crisp; transfer the waffle to the warmed baking sheet. Repeat with the remaining batter.

❹ Top the warm waffles with the avocado slices, a squeeze of lemon juice, and hemp seeds; season with salt and pepper.

Chipotle Queso Dip ⓥ

MAKES: 2 CUPS // **SERVES:** 6 TO 8 // **PREP TIME:** 12 HOURS // **COOK TIME:** 1 TO 2 MINUTES

With certain sports events taking place in the month of February, I thought it only fitting to include a vegan dip that tastes so strikingly close to an original cheese dip that you question whether it's even good for you—but surprisingly it's packed with nutrients. The chickpea flour and cashew base provide that warm, creamy consistency that's so unmistakable in a queso dip, while the nutritional yeast gives it that cheesy quality and the turmeric gives it a vibrant color. Traditional tortilla chips, crackers, or cut vegetable spears are all great to enjoy with this dip.

½ cup (80 g) raw cashews, soaked overnight and drained

2 garlic cloves, roughly chopped

1 shallot, roughly chopped

¼ cup (34 g) jarred jalapeños

2 tablespoons nutritional yeast

¼ to ½ teaspoon ground turmeric

1 tablespoon jalapeño juice (from the jar)

½ teaspoon sea salt

¼ teaspoon chipotle powder (or chili powder)

1 cup (240 ml) water

¼ cup (30 g) chickpea flour

½ ripe avocado, cut into small chunks

Handful of grape or cherry tomatoes, halved

2 tablespoons chopped cilantro

❶ In a high-speed blender, blend the cashews, garlic, shallot, jalapeños, yeast, ¼ teaspoon turmeric, jalapeño juice, salt, and chipotle powder; set aside.

❷ In a small saucepan, whisk together the water and chickpea flour until no lumps remain. Turn the heat to medium and continue whisking every few seconds to prevent scorching. Whisk for roughly 6 to 7 minutes, until the mixture thickens and resembles a roux or melted cheese. Remove from the heat and carefully scrape into the blender with the other ingredients.

❸ Blend the ingredients on high for 1 minute, stopping to scrape down the sides of the blender, until smooth and creamy. Taste and adjust seasoning, adding more chipotle, salt, turmeric, or yeast if desired.

❹ Use a rubber spatula to scrape the dip into a serving bowl, and top with the avocado, tomatoes, and cilantro; serve immediately while hot, or let dip cool a bit (dip will continue to thicken as it cools).

❺ Leftovers can be refrigerated in a resealable container and can be eaten cold or reheated on the stove.

Mini Polenta Pizzas
with Caramelized Fennel and Garlic Paste ⓥ

MAKES: 9 PIZZAS // **SERVES:** 4 TO 6 // **PREP TIME:** 45 MINUTES TO 1 HOUR // **COOK TIME:** 20 MINUTES

Chickpea flour is a wonderful replacement for polenta. Polenta, when cooked for a longer period of time, becomes stiff and able to hold a shape. The same goes for chickpea flour when cooked on the stovetop. It's then dolloped into small rounds, baked in the oven, and topped with sweet roasted garlic and crisp caramelized fennel. These are great to serve as appetizers, but are hearty enough for a dinner meal.

1 head of garlic

3 tablespoons plus 2 teaspoons extra virgin olive oil

Coarse sea salt

1 cup (120 g) chickpea flour

1 tablespoon nutritional yeast

½ teaspoon sea salt, plus more to taste

1 teaspoon chopped sage

1 teaspoon chopped thyme

2 cups (480 ml) vegetable broth

½ teaspoon lemon juice

½ teaspoon lemon zest (about ½ lemon)

½ teaspoon chopped rosemary

Pinch of red pepper flakes

2 fennel bulbs, trimmed and sliced thin, fronds reserved

① Preheat oven to 400°F (200°C). Cut the top of the garlic off, about a ¼ inch, exposing the tops of the cloves, and peel a few of the papery layers away; place in foil and drizzle liberally with olive oil (about 2 teaspoons) and sprinkle with coarse salt. Fold up sides and make a packet; roast for 40 to 45 minutes, until soft and mushy. Remove from the oven and let cool. Keep the oven on for the pizzas.

② Prepare a baking sheet with parchment and set aside.

③ Make the polenta. In a saucepan, whisk together flour, yeast, salt, sage, and thyme; then whisk in the broth. Turn the heat to medium, and continue whisking until no lumps remain. Cook until the mixture thickens. At this point trade the whisk for a wooden spoon or rubber spatula and keep stirring, scraping the bottom and sides of the pan to avoid scorching. Cook until the mixture resembles a thick batter and pulls away from the sides of the pan, about 15 to 20 minutes.

④ Spoon the polenta onto the prepared baking sheet, flattening with the back of a spoon into 3- to 4-inch rounds; then transfer the polenta crusts to the refrigerator for 15 minutes to cool.

⑤ Make the garlic paste. Squeeze the roasted garlic from the skins into a mortar; add the lemon juice, lemon zest, rosemary, 2 tablespoons oil, and red pepper flakes; season with salt and mash into a smooth paste. Set aside.

⑥ Remove polenta crusts from the refrigerator and bake for 20 minutes, until edges are lightly browned.

⑦ Add the remaining 1 tablespoon oil to a skillet over medium heat. Add the sliced fennel and cook, stirring every few minutes, until lightly browned and caramelized, about 15 minutes. Set aside.

⑧ Smooth the garlic paste over the top of the crusts and place back in the oven; cook for 5 minutes, until the paste is warmed through and fragrant.

⑨ Remove the polenta pizzas from the oven and transfer to a plate; spread the caramelized fennel on the top of crusts, and garnish with the reserved fennel fronds. Serve warm.

Flatbread with Harissa, Kale, and Gaeta Olives ⓥ

MAKES: 1 LARGE FLATBREAD // **PREP TIME:** 25 MINUTES // **COOK TIME:** 10 TO 12 MINUTES

This is a simple and quick flatbread recipe—great for weeknights, as a snack, or as a companion to any dip you might have in your refrigerator. The combination of harissa, kale, and olives is flavorful, hearty, and a bit spicy—use more or less harissa depending on how much spice you want. While this flatbread can be a base for just about anything you want to top it with, I love it with this combination of flavors this time of year to break up the recurring root vegetable of the season.

1 cup (120 g) chickpea flour

½ teaspoon sea salt

Freshly ground pepper

1 tablespoon plus 2 teaspoons extra virgin olive oil

1 tablespoon coconut milk

2 to 3 tablespoons water

Sorghum flour, for dusting

2 to 3 tablespoons harissa paste

1 garlic clove, minced

4 to 5 large kale leaves, roughly chopped

1 teaspoon red wine vinegar

¼ cup (45 g) pitted Gaeta olives, roughly chopped (or substitute Kalamata)

1 tablespoon toasted pine nuts

❶ In a large bowl, whisk together the chickpea flour, salt, and pepper. Drizzle in 1 tablespoon of oil and the milk and use your hands to mix together until crumbly. One tablespoon at a time, mix the water in and use your hands to distribute until you have a smooth, uniform dough. Knead the dough for 5 minutes, until soft and springy. Place under a damp dish towel for 10 minutes.

❷ Place a baking stone in the oven and preheat to 400°F (200°C); dust a large piece of parchment with sorghum flour. Use a rolling pin to roll the dough into a large oval with a ⅛-inch thickness, turning and dusting the dough to prevent sticking.

❸ Using a pizza peel (or a cookie sheet), transfer the dough to the hot stone. Bake for 4 minutes; remove the dough with a pizza peel (or a cookie sheet) and spread the harissa paste over the top. Use the peel once more to transfer the flatbread back to the oven. Cook for another 6 to 8 minutes, until edges are crisp and golden.

❹ While the dough is cooking, sauté the kale. Heat 2 teaspoons of oil in a skillet over medium heat. Once the pan is hot, add the garlic and stir; cook until fragrant, about 30 seconds. Add the kale and vinegar, and stir; cook until leaves wilt and turn dark green, about 1 minute. Remove from the heat and toss together with the olives and pine nuts (reserve a few pine nuts for garnish).

❺ Top the flatbread with the kale mixture and leftover pine nuts; serve warm.

Acorn Squash Tart with Caramelized Onions and Collard Greens ⓥ

MAKES: ONE 9-INCH TART // **SERVES:** 8 // **PREP TIME:** 40 MINUTES // **COOK TIME:** 25 MINUTES

Whenever my husband and I have friends or family over I constantly try to cook something that's gluten-free, vegan, allergy-free, filling, and tasty! It's not always easy to meet all criteria, but this tart hits the mark. It's one I come back to often because it's easy to make ahead of time and to reheat when you're ready to serve. Guests will leave happy and full. Thanks to the chickpea flour base, this tart is packed with protein and can truly stand up as a full dinner meal. Switch up the winter squash depending on what you have available to you: acorn and delicata squash can both be used because their skins' texture offers a beautiful, scalloped design. However, peeled butternut squash or even kabocha squash would be just as delicious.

FILLING

1 large acorn squash (or 2 small, about 1,000 g)

2 tablespoons extra virgin olive oil

1 teaspoon balsamic vinegar

1 teaspoon thyme, plus a few sprigs for garnish

¼ teaspoon red pepper flakes

Coarse sea salt and freshly ground pepper

1 large onion, halved and sliced into thin half-moons

1 garlic clove, minced

3 cups (135 g) roughly chopped collard greens

CRUST

1¼ cups (150 g) chickpea flour, plus more for dusting

1 tablespoon arrowroot powder

½ teaspoon sea salt

⅛ teaspoon freshly ground pepper

2 tablespoons extra virgin olive oil

4 to 5 tablespoons water

❶ Preheat oven to 375°F (190°C) and line a baking sheet with parchment paper; set aside. Trim the ends of the squash, cut in half, and then cut each piece in half so you have four pieces. Slice the squash into ¼-inch pieces; place in a large bowl.

❷ Combine the squash, 1 tablespoon of oil, vinegar, thyme, chili flakes, and salt and pepper, to taste. Transfer to the prepared baking sheet and bake in the oven until tender, about 30 minutes. Remove from the oven and set aside. (Turn the temperature up to 400°F/200°C for the tart crust.)

❸ While squash is cooking, heat a skillet over medium heat and add the remaining tablespoon of oil. Once pan is hot, add the onion and a few pinches of salt; stir every few minutes until lightly browned and caramelized, about 15 to 20 minutes. Remove onion from the pan, and turn the heat to medium-low; add the garlic and cook for 30 seconds (if your pan looks dry, add a bit more oil to coat). Add the collards and a couple pinches of salt; cook until wilted, about 1 to 2 minutes; remove from the heat and mix with caramelized onions. Set aside.

❹ Grease a 9-inch tart pan and set aside. To make the crust, in a large mixing bowl whisk together the flour, arrowroot, salt, and pepper. Add the oil and use your hands or a fork to work into the flour until crumbly. One tablespoon at a time, add the water and use your hands or a fork to distribute and mix until the dough comes together and is smooth; it should take approximately 4 tablespoons to achieve this, but if your dough is crumbly or cracking, add up to 1 tablespoon more water. Knead the dough for about 5 minutes, until smooth, then let the dough rest while you prepare a clean work surface.

❺ Place a large piece of parchment paper on an even work surface and dust it generously with flour. Dust the dough and rolling pin, and roll out to an 11-inch round, turning and dusting the dough to make sure it doesn't stick to the parchment. If the dough tears, simply pinch it back together. Carefully transfer the dough to the prepared tart pan and push the dough into the sides of the pan and trim any extra dough hanging over; use a fork to prick the bottom of the crust and bake for 6 to 8 minutes, until edges are lightly golden.

⓺ Remove from the oven, lower temperature to 375°F (190°C), and fill the tart with the caramelized onions, then the collards. Finally, arrange the squash pieces skin side up, moving from the outside of the pan to the inside, overlapping a bit until you reach the middle. Place the filled tart back in the oven and bake until warmed through and crust is lightly brown and golden, 10 to 15 minutes.

⓻ Top with leftover thyme sprigs and serve warm.

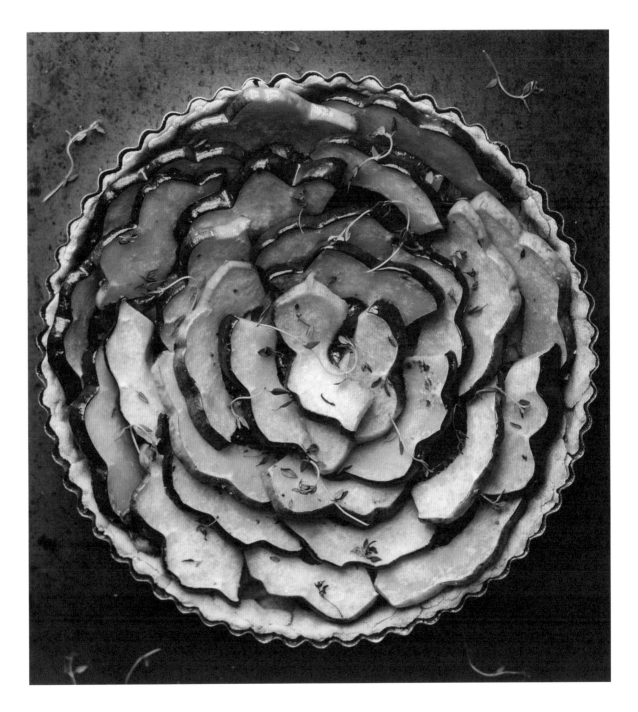

Chocolate Olive Oil Cakes
with Chocolate Glaze

MAKES: 8 MINI CAKES // **PREP TIME:** 10 MINUTES // **COOK TIME:** 20 TO 25 MINUTES

These mini cakes are rich and moist and a perfect single-serve dessert. They're even more delicious when served with a dollop of coconut cream or coconut milk–vanilla bean ice cream. Add some pomegranate seeds or sliced blood orange for a festive Valentine's Day dessert. (If you don't own mini Bundt pans, you can use an 8-inch Bundt pan for one 8-inch round cake, bake for 35 to 40 minutes, and use the same amount of chocolate drizzle for topping the cake as well.)

CHOCOLATE CAKES

1 cup (144 g) coconut sugar

¾ cup (90 g) chickpea flour

½ cup (70 g) brown rice flour

¼ cup (30 g) arrowroot powder

¼ cup (20 g) raw cacao powder, plus extra for dusting

1 teaspoon baking powder

½ teaspoon baking soda

½ teaspoon sea salt

2 large eggs

1 cup (240 ml) almond milk

¼ cup (60 ml) extra virgin olive oil

1½ teaspoons pure vanilla extract

CHOCOLATE DRIZZLE

½ cup (60 g) chopped bittersweet chocolate (preferably 60 to 70 percent cacao)

2 teaspoons coconut oil

1 Preheat oven to 350°F (180°C). Grease eight mini Bundt pans and place them on a rimmed baking sheet; set aside.

2 In a large mixing bowl, whisk together the dry ingredients; set aside. In a medium bowl, whisk together the eggs, milk, olive oil, and vanilla. Whisk the wet ingredients into the dry and mix until smooth.

3 Divide the batter among the molds, and bake for 20 to 25 minutes, until a cake tester inserted into the center comes out clean.

4 Transfer the baking sheet to a rack and let cool for 30 minutes. Once cool enough to handle, invert the cakes onto a platter and let cool completely.

5 Melt the chocolate in a heatproof bowl over simmering water until melted; stir in the coconut oil until thoroughly combined. Spoon the glaze over top of each cake and allow it to cool and harden at room temperature.

Fresh Ginger and Pomegranate Muffins

MAKES: 12 MUFFINS // **PREP TIME:** 10 MINUTES // **COOK TIME:** 25 MINUTES

Weekend mornings in the winter can often feel so slow. You pull the sheets back ever so gently to minimize the amount of cold air rushing toward you, deliberately taking your time from the bed to the kitchen to make a pot of coffee, and thoughtfully choosing what to make to brighten your home with the scent of spiced baked goods. Most times, I make a muffin recipe because I usually have all the ingredients on hand, and I can incorporate whatever seasonal fruit I have around. Ginger and pomegranates are staples in my kitchen during the colder months, and they complement each other perfectly in just about any form. These muffins are best when eaten within 2 days but can be stored in an airtight container for up to 4 days.

1 cup (120 g) chickpea flour

½ cup (70 g) brown rice flour

½ cup (57 g) oat flour

⅔ cup (96 g) coconut sugar

1½ teaspoons baking powder

1 teaspoon freshly grated ginger

½ teaspoon baking soda

½ teaspoon ground cinnamon

½ teaspoon ground nutmeg

½ teaspoon sea salt

2 large eggs

½ cup (120 ml) almond milk

½ cup (120 ml) sunflower oil

1 teaspoon pure vanilla extract

½ cup (85 g) pomegranate seeds

Chopped almonds (optional)

❶ Preheat oven to 350°F (180°C) and line a twelve-cup muffin pan with liners. Set aside.

❷ In a large bowl, whisk together the flours, sugar, baking powder, ginger, baking soda, cinnamon, nutmeg, and salt. In another large bowl, combine the eggs, milk, oil, and vanilla. Gradually add the dry ingredients into the wet, using a rubber spatula to mix. Fold the pomegranate seeds into the batter, reserving a few for the tops of the muffins. Divide the batter among the muffin cups and top with the reserved pomegranate seeds and chopped almonds.

❸ Bake in the center of the oven for 25 minutes, until a cake tester inserted into the center of a muffin comes out clean and muffins are golden.

❹ Let the muffins cool for 10 minutes, then remove them from the tin and allow to cool completely before serving.

Irish Soda Bread

MAKES: ONE 6-INCH ROUND LOAF // **SERVES:** 6 TO 8 // **PREP TIME:** 10 MINUTES
COOK TIME: 40 TO 45 MINUTES

My grandmother's ancestors came to New York City following Ireland's potato famine, so Irish soda bread for Saint Patrick's Day has been a food staple in my family since I was a child. There wasn't any family recipe passed down; rather, we would pick up a loaf from a local bakery and bring it to my nana's house to enjoy with a good schmear of butter. Over the years, I've been making a gluten-free version of soda bread using a vegan buttermilk mixture to achieve a similar taste to traditional soda bread. The chickpea flour provides the bread with a sturdiness that is always needed in gluten-free baking, and the oat flour is added to make the bread a bit more tender. I personally prefer dried currants to raisins and crushed caraway seeds to whole seeds, since I find they create a subtler outcome.

¾ cup (180 ml) coconut milk

1 tablespoon apple cider vinegar

1 cup (120 g) chickpea flour

1 cup (114 g) oat flour, plus more for dusting

2 tablespoons cane sugar

1 teaspoon psyllium husk powder

1½ teaspoons baking soda

½ teaspoon baking powder

½ teaspoon sea salt

½ teaspoon crushed caraway seeds

1 large egg

¼ cup (40 g) dried currants

Oil for your hands

❶ Preheat oven to 375°F (190°C) and line a baking sheet with parchment paper; set aside.

❷ In a small bowl, combine the milk and vinegar; let the mixture sit for 10 minutes until top is bubbly.

❸ While the mixture is sitting, whisk together the flours, sugar, psyllium powder, baking soda, baking powder, salt, and caraway. When the milk and vinegar mixture is ready, add the egg, whisking until combined. Using a rubber spatula, add the wet ingredients to the dry and fold the ingredients together; then fold in the currants. Lightly oil your hands and gather the dough into a ball, place on the prepared baking sheet, and flatten into a disk, about 1 inch.

❹ Bake the bread for 40 to 45 minutes, rotating halfway through for even baking, until golden.

❺ Let the bread cool completely before slicing. Bread can be stored at room temperature covered with parchment paper. It will continue to dry out each day it's left out and should last about 3 days.

Chickpea Frites with Sriracha Ketchup ⓥ

SERVES: 4 AS A SNACK // **PREP TIME:** 4 TO 12 HOURS // **COOK TIME:** 25 MINUTES

When I first heard of chickpea fries I never could have imagined how delicious they would be. They mimic a potato french fry almost completely but with less grease and more protein. There are a few ways to make them, but my favorite is to fry them small-batch style, taking care not to overcrowd the pan, and letting each frite get golden brown and crunchy. Don't be overwhelmed by the preparation time, as it accounts for time in the refrigerator letting the chickpea mixture thicken and congeal. Once the rest period is over, the only work left is to slice and fry them. Like potato frites, these are best eaten hot and fresh.

FRITES

2 cups (480 ml) water

1 cup (120 g) chickpea flour

1 teaspoon sea salt,
plus more to taste

⅛ teaspoon freshly ground pepper

½ cup (120 ml) sunflower oil

SRIRACHA KETCHUP

½ cup (120 g) ketchup

2 teaspoons sriracha

❶ Lightly grease an 8 x 8-inch rectangular pan, or another pan of a similar size. Set aside.

❷ In a saucepan, whisk together the water, flour, salt, and pepper, until no lumps remain. Turn the heat to medium and continue whisking until mixture thickens, about 6 to 7 minutes. Remove from the heat and pour in the prepared pan. Use a rubber spatula to spread the mixture out evenly. Let the mixture cool at room temperature, and refrigerate at least 4 hours or overnight.

❸ Make the sriracha ketchup. Whisk together the ketchup and sriracha, cover with plastic wrap, and refrigerate until ready to use.

❹ Slice the cooled chickpea mixture into ¼-inch slices; then slice in half.

❺ Generously coat the bottom of a skillet with ¼ cup of oil, and heat over medium, until hot and shimmering. In batches, add the frites to the pan, making sure not to overcrowd them. Cook for 2 minutes, and turn the frites over, cooking all sides until lightly browned and crisp. Transfer to a paper towel–lined plate and repeat with the remaining frites, adding more oil as needed.

❻ Serve hot with sriracha ketchup. Top with salt as desired.

Chickpea Banh Mi ⓥ

MAKES: 8 SANDWICHES // PREP TIME: 12 HOURS // COOK TIME: 15 MINUTES

Ordinarily, you may have seen a vegetarian version of a banh mi made with marinated tofu. The idea here is similar, but a chickpea flour–based filling is what's at the center of this sandwich. Its marinade is full of spice and umami flavor, and it's topped with lightly pickled vegetables and aromatic herbs to deepen the flavors even more.

CHICKPEA FILLING

2 cups (480 ml) water

1 cup (120 g) chickpea flour

½ teaspoon fine sea salt

Freshly ground pepper

2 tablespoons sunflower oil

PICKLED VEGETABLES

½ cup (120 ml) apple cider vinegar

2 teaspoons maple syrup

½ teaspoon fine sea salt

4 radishes, sliced paper-thin

1 cucumber, sliced thin lengthwise

2 small carrots, julienned

MARINADE

1 tablespoon gluten-free mellow white miso

1 tablespoon extra virgin olive oil

2 teaspoons sriracha

2 teaspoons gluten-free tamari

2 garlic cloves, smashed

Juice of 1 lime

SRIRACHA MAYO

½ cup (124 g) Vegenaise

2 tablespoons sriracha

2 to 3 teaspoons maple syrup

2 teaspoons gluten-free tamari

½ teaspoon lime juice

Gluten-free baguettes

¼ cup (15 g) chopped cilantro

¼ cup (15 g) shiso or Thai basil leaves

❶ Lightly grease an 8 x 8-inch square dish and set aside.

❷ Make the chickpea filling. In a small saucepan, whisk together the water, flour, salt, and pepper, to taste, until no lumps remain. Turn the heat to medium and continue whisking until mixture thickens. When it thickens, place the whisk aside and use a rubber spatula or wooden spoon. Keep stirring until the chickpea mixture pulls away from the sides of the pan, about 6 to 7 minutes.

❸ Quickly transfer the mixture to the prepared dish and use the back of a spatula to smooth into an even layer. Let cool completely, then cover loosely with plastic wrap and refrigerate at least 4 hours or overnight.

❹ While the chickpea filling is in the refrigerator, prepare the pickled vegetables. Whisk together the vinegar, syrup, and salt until dissolved. Place vegetables in a jar or shallow bowl and pour pickling juice over top; if pickling juice doesn't cover the vegetables, add water to cover. Set aside for 30 minutes, then drain and rinse the vegetables. Place in a lidded jar or airtight container and refrigerate the vegetables until ready to use.

❺ Remove the chickpea filling from the refrigerator, invert onto a large cutting board, and slice into eight pieces (or cut according to how big your bread is); place on a paper towel to soak up any residual water. Place the pieces in a shallow dish. To marinate the chickpea filling, whisk together the marinade ingredients in a bowl and brush over the tops and bottoms of the sliced chickpea pieces.

❻ Coat the bottom of a skillet with roughly 2 tablespoons of oil and heat over medium, until the oil is hot and shimmering. Fry the chickpea filling in batches, until both sides are golden brown, about 1 to 2 minutes on each side. Transfer to a paper towel–lined plate and repeat with the remaining pieces, adding more cooking oil as needed.

❼ Whisk together the sriracha mayo ingredients; set aside. Slice the bread in half, spread the sriracha mayo over both sides, place one chickpea fritter on top, and then top with pickled vegetables, cilantro, and shiso (or basil).

Spiced Black Bean Tostadas
with Kiwi Salsa ⓥ

MAKES: 8 TOSTADAS // **PREP TIME:** 40 MINUTES // **COOK TIME:** 25 MINUTES

If there was ever a bright, hearty late-winter meal, this is it! It's one of my and my husband's go-to dinners. While there's a bit of preparation involved, it's totally worth it. The tostada base is made purely of chickpea flour. They are pan-fried in a dry skillet and then charred a bit over a flame for added flavor. The tostadas are then topped with quick and very tasty five-spice black beans and a kiwi-tomatillo salsa that refreshes the entire dish.

SALSA

¼ cup (40 g) diced red onion

Juice of ½ lime

2 kiwis, peeled and diced

1 large tomatillo, husked, rinsed and diced

½ jalapeño, seeded and minced

¼ cup (15 g) finely chopped cilantro

1 teaspoon extra virgin olive oil

Pinch of sea salt

TOSTADA

2 cups (240 g) chickpea flour

½ teaspoon sea salt

Freshly ground pepper

2 tablespoons coconut milk

2 tablespoons extra virgin olive oil

¼ to ½ cup (60 to 120 ml) water*

Sorghum flour, for dusting

FIVE-SPICE BLACK BEANS

1 tablespoon extra virgin olive oil

1 shallot, finely diced

2 garlic cloves, minced

One 15-ounce (425 g) can black beans

½ to ¾ teaspoon fine sea salt

1½ teaspoons ground cumin

1 teaspoon chili powder

1 teaspoon raw cacao powder

½ teaspoon ground cinnamon

Pinch of cayenne (optional)

❶ Toss together the onion and lime juice in a bowl; set aside for 10 minutes. Toss together the softened onions, kiwis, tomatillo, jalapeño, cilantro, oil, and salt. Set aside or refrigerate until ready to use.

❷ Make the tostadas. Whisk together the chickpea flour, salt, and pepper, to taste. Add the milk and oil; use your hands to mix until crumbly. Drizzle in the water a tablespoon at a time until the dough is smooth. Knead for 5 minutes; if the dough is cracking in places, dampen your hands as needed and continue to knead until smooth.

❸ Form the dough into a ball and let it rest under a damp paper towel for 10 minutes. Place a large piece of parchment over a work surface and dust with sorghum flour. Divide the dough into two even balls and then divide each piece into four even pieces, giving you eight pieces.

❹ Heat a skillet over medium heat.

❺ Roll out the balls into 4- to 5-inch rounds, dusting and turning to prevent sticking. Place a tostada into the dry skillet and cook for about 1 minute, until you see white bubbles form on top of the dough; flip over and cook for another 45 seconds to 1 minute. Heat a gas stovetop with a medium-low flame; using tongs, toast the tostadas, rotating and flipping them until charred in places. Set aside. (If you don't have a gas stove, continue cooking the tostadas in the skillet, flipping them until crisp.)

❻ To make the black beans, heat the oil in a skillet over medium heat. Once hot, add the shallot; stir and cook until soft and translucent, about 2 minutes. Add the garlic and stir; cook for 30 seconds, until fragrant. Add the entire can of black beans (including the liquid), salt, and spices. Cook until the liquid has thickened and reduced to half, about 8 to 10 minutes. Taste and adjust salt and spices, if needed.

❼ Top the tostada shells with black beans and salsa.

*Note: The amount of water used depends on certain variables. Start with ¼ cup and then drizzle in more water as you need to obtain a smooth dough.

Mung Bean Pancakes
with Carrots, Scallions, and Ginger

SERVES: 4 // **PREP TIME:** 15 MINUTES // **COOK TIME:** 30 MINUTES

There are many variations of Korean pancakes. These are an adaptation of *bindaedok*, which are made with split mung beans (sold as moong dal in many grocery stores) and have large ribbons of carrots throughout the pancake. These serve wonderfully at lunch and are also filling enough for dinner. March farmers' markets can be pretty barren, but carrots are still plentiful, making them the perfect center for this comforting meal.

DIPPING SAUCE

1 tablespoon rice vinegar

2 teaspoons toasted sesame oil

1 teaspoon maple syrup

½ teaspoon gluten-free tamari

2 tablespoons sliced scallions

1 garlic clove, minced

Freshly ground pepper

1 teaspoon toasted sesame seeds

PANCAKES

1 cup (192 g) moong dal or split mung beans, soaked for 4 hours or overnight

1 cup (240 ml) water

3 tablespoons chickpea flour

1 egg

3 garlic cloves, roughly chopped

1 teaspoon Korean chili powder

1 teaspoon sea salt

One 1-inch piece of ginger, peeled and minced

½ teaspoon gluten-free tamari

½ teaspoon rice wine vinegar

2 carrots, julienned and roughly chopped

1 bunch scallions, trimmed and sliced thin, plus more for garnish

2 tablespoons chopped cilantro, 2 tablespoons extra virgin olive oil

❶ Whisk together the vinegar, oil, syrup, tamari, scallions, garlic, and pepper, to taste. Taste and adjust. Stir in the sesame seeds and set aside.

❷ To make the pancakes, place the soaked beans in an upright high-speed blender with the water, flour, egg, garlic, chili powder, salt, ginger, tamari, and vinegar; blend on high until combined, about 30 seconds. Transfer the batter to a large bowl and fold in the carrots, scallions, and cilantro.

❸ Heat the oil in a 10-inch skillet over medium heat. Drop 2 heaping tablespoons worth of batter for each pancake; cook for 4 to 5 minutes, until golden brown, flip over, and cook for another 2 minutes, until golden. Transfer cooked pancakes to a paper towel–lined plate to soak up any extra oil. Repeat with remaining batter, adding more cooking oil, if needed.

❹ Plate the pancakes, top with extra scallions, and serve with a side of dipping sauce.

Sweet Crepes with Kumquat Marmalade

MAKES: 1 CUP MARMALADE AND TEN 8-INCH CREPES // **SERVES:** 8 // **PREP TIME:** 30 MINUTES
COOK TIME: 15 MINUTES

Crepes are quite possibly the most versatile food. Whether you're making sweet or savory crepes, breakfast or dinner crepes, they're a wonderful vessel for all types of meals. Crepes are a big deal here in New York City, where you can find every type of crepe imaginable. However, the crepes I tend to love the most are sweet ones that incorporate some form of seasonal fruit, whether it's a jam, compote, or diced. Like other citrus fruits, kumquats are available in the winter. The beauty of these slightly sour fruits: no need to peel them—the skin is the best part!

CREPES

1 cup (120 g) chickpea flour

2 tablespoons cane sugar

¼ teaspoon sea salt

1 cup (240 ml) almond milk

2 large eggs

MARMALADE

1 pound (456 g) kumquats

¼ cup plus 1 to 2 tablespoons raw honey

2 tablespoons fresh orange juice

2 tablespoons water

Pinch of sea salt

½ teaspoon coconut oil

❶ In a large bowl, whisk together the flour, sugar, and salt; whisk in the milk and eggs until incorporated. Let the mixture rest in the refrigerator for 30 minutes.

❷ While the crepe batter is resting, make the marmalade. Slice the kumquats; place in a small saucepan with the honey, orange juice, water, and salt. Bring to a simmer and cook, stirring every so often, until the jam has thickened and the kumquats have fallen apart, about 10 to 12 minutes. Turn the heat off and allow the mixture to cool.

❸ Remove the batter from the refrigerator, and heat the coconut oil in a 10-inch skillet over medium heat. Once the pan is hot, scoop a scant ¼ cup of the batter onto the skillet, giving it a swirl so that it forms a large circle, roughly 8 inches in diameter. Cook for 1 minute, until bubbles appear in the center and on the sides; flip over and cook for another 30 seconds. Repeat with the remaining batter, adding more oil as needed.

❹ Top the crepes with marmalade and serve warm.

Almond Butter Brownies

MAKES: 16 BROWNIES // **PREP TIME:** 15 MINUTES // **COOK TIME:** 20 TO 25 MINUTES

Boxed brownies were the first things I remember baking when I was growing up. Sometimes my mom would allow me to buy the chocolate chip brownie mix and, on special occasions, the fudge brownie mix. But as soon as I got old enough to make brownies from scratch, I would buy the best dark chocolate I could find at the grocery store and fold it into the batter, reserving some for the top, along with a good amount of chopped nuts. Dark chocolate always provides the most rich and luscious brownies without giving me a toothache. These brownies incorporate melted and chunked dark chocolate as well as creamy almond butter for a chewy brownie.

⅓ cup (40 g) chickpea flour

½ teaspoon baking soda

½ teaspoon sea salt

6 ounces (170 g) bittersweet chocolate (65 to 70 percent cacao), roughly chopped

1 cup (144 g) coconut sugar

2 large eggs

1 cup (240 g) almond butter

1 teaspoon pure vanilla extract

½ cup (50 g) chopped almonds (optional)

❶ Preheat oven to 350°F (180°C) and grease an 8 x 8-inch square pan. Line the pan with parchment paper and allow two sides to hang over like wings; set aside.

❷ In a small bowl, whisk together the flour, baking soda, and salt; set aside.

❸ In a heatproof bowl, melt 4 ounces of the chocolate, reserving the other 2 ounces for topping; stir until completely melted. Set aside to cool for a couple minutes.

❹ In a large bowl, whisk together the sugar and eggs; whisk in the almond butter and vanilla. Then pour in the melted chocolate and mix; fold in the flour mixture and mix until combined; the mixture will be thick and gooey.

❺ Pour the batter into the prepared pan, smooth out the top with a rubber spatula, and sprinkle the remaining chocolate and chopped almonds. Bake for 20 to 25 minutes (I like to err on the undercooked side because brownies that are overcooked can get very dry. When testing brownies for doneness, some of the brownie should stick to the toothpick).

❻ Allow the brownies to cool for 20 minutes. Using the parchment wings, lift the brownies from the pan, transfer to a rack and let cool completely. Slice the brownies into squares.

❼ Brownies can be stored in an airtight container at room temperature for up to 4 days.

Spring Months

Spring is that season that bursts with life after the deep stillness of winter. Everything is reinvigorated, from tender green buds on tree branches to the first onions shooting up through the earth's surface; it's the time of year when nature's life cycle is most unmistakable. Here in New York, fresh herbs, spring garlic, and spring onions most notoriously mark the beginnings of spring. At Union Square Greenmarket, the largest market the city has, there are lines of people waiting to get their hands on ramps, a wild leek that's the season's first little alliums, which are distinctly marked by their small, pinkish-white bulbs and their long tender leaves. Then come the stalks of tart red rhubarb, leafy broccoli rabe, colorful herb flowers, peppery radishes, and those not-to-be-missed sweet, juicy strawberries. April, May, and June are all about celebrating the beginning, middle, and end of spring by rejoicing in what each month has to offer.

Clumpy Granola Bowl
with Stewed Rhubarb and Yogurt ⓥ

MAKES: 3 CUPS OF GRANOLA // **SERVES:** 4 // **PREP TIME:** 10 MINUTES // **COOK TIME:** 40 TO 45 MINUTES

I didn't really understand the lure of clumpy granola until I started making my own at home. Many recipes for a clumpier granola call for egg whites to bind the various ingredients together. While I've tried the egg white version in the past, what I really love is adding flour to the mix, helping the ingredients adhere to one another in a way similar to a fruit crumble topping. The chickpea flour here adds a good dose of protein to your morning routine as well as a lovely nutty flavor from being baked and toasted at a low heat. Aside from eating granola with milk, I add it to some stewed fruit—in this case, rhubarb—and coconut yogurt. It's a slightly decadent, but wholesome, way to start the day.

GRANOLA

2 cups (210 g) gluten-free
old-fashioned rolled oats

½ cup (85 g) almonds, chopped

½ cup (15 g) puffed brown rice

½ cup (60 g) chickpea flour

¼ cup (33 g) pumpkin seeds

¼ cup (35 g) sunflower seeds

1 teaspoon ground cinnamon

1 teaspoon ground ginger

½ teaspoon ground nutmeg

½ teaspoon sea salt

⅓ cup (80 ml) maple syrup

¼ cup (60 ml) coconut oil, melted

STEWED RHUBARB

1 rhubarb stalk, trimmed and cut
into 1-inch pieces

1 tablespoon maple syrup

1 teaspoon lemon juice

½ vanilla bean pod, scraped (or ½
teaspoon pure vanilla extract)

1 cup (250 g) coconut yogurt (or
yogurt of choice)

❶ Preheat oven to 300°F (150°C) and line a baking sheet with parchment paper; set aside.

❷ In a large bowl, whisk together all the dry ingredients until thoroughly combined. In a small bowl, whisk together the syrup and oil, and then fold into the dry mix with a wooden spoon or rubber spatula. Mix for 2 to 3 minutes, until the granola is wet and clumpy.

❸ Transfer the granola to the prepared baking sheet and use the back of your spoon or spatula to spread it out in an even layer.

❹ Bake for 40 to 45 minutes, rotating halfway through, until lightly browned and fragrant. Remove from the oven; let cool completely. Gently break up the granola into clumps and store in an airtight container at room temperature for up to 2 weeks.

❺ To make the stewed rhubarb, heat a small saucepan over medium-low heat; add the rhubarb, syrup, lemon juice, and vanilla bean, and stir. Cook for 6 to 8 minutes, until bubbling and the rhubarb is tender and loses a bit of its color. Remove from the heat and set aside.

❻ Divide the yogurt among four bowls, add a ½ cup of granola to each bowl (there will be 1 cup granola left over), and then divide the stewed rhubarb among the bowls.

Mango Poppy Seed Cornmeal Muffins

MAKES: 12 MUFFINS // **PREP TIME:** 10 MINUTES // **COOK TIME:** 25 MINUTES

When my husband and I were dating he would often take me to his neighborhood coffee shop in the West Village for some morning fuel and a bite to eat. While the coffee was great, their muffins were what really kept me coming back. Each morning they would arrange the muffins behind their case, and I would read the flavors to myself, not knowing which one to pick—they all sounded so good! But there was one muffin I kept going back to: a corn muffin studded with warm, tender mango. I never would have thought of incorporating fruit in a corn bread–like muffin. This recipe is a take on the original, but with more mango and some poppy seeds for added flecks of crunch.

1 cup (120 g) chickpea flour

1 cup (133 g) stone-ground cornmeal

⅔ cup (96 g) cane sugar

2 teaspoons poppy seeds

1½ teaspoons baking powder

½ teaspoon baking soda

½ teaspoon sea salt

2 large eggs

½ cup (120 ml) sunflower oil

½ cup (120 ml) almond milk

1 teaspoon pure vanilla extract

½ ripe but firm mango, peeled and diced into ¼-inch chunks

❶ Preheat oven to 350°F (180°C) and line a twelve-cup muffin pan with liners; set aside.

❷ In a large bowl, whisk together all the dry ingredients. In another large bowl, whisk together the eggs and oil until pale yellow. Add the milk and vanilla and whisk to incorporate. In thirds, add the dry ingredients to the wet, and whisk until mixed.

❸ Fill the muffin liners halfway; divide the mango evenly among the muffins. Then fill with remaining batter. Bake for 25 minutes, until a cake tester inserted into the center of a muffin comes out clean.

❹ Let the muffins cool for 10 minutes, then remove them from the tin and allow to cool a few minutes more before serving warm.

Skillet Spinach and Chive Quiche

SERVES: 6 TO 8 // **PREP TIME:** 25 MINUTES // **COOK TIME:** 35 TO 40 MINUTES

Here chickpea flour becomes a wonderful gluten-free crust for quiche. It lends a lovely nutty flavor and aroma you can't find with other flours. Using a cast-iron skillet makes all the difference; it gently toasts and cooks the crust, giving it that nutty flavor while also making it look crisp—this dish will impress, especially if you're serving it for brunch. Leftovers can be stored in the refrigerator for up to 2 days and reheated as desired.

FILLING

6 large eggs

2 cups (40 g) baby spinach, roughly chopped

½ cup (120 ml) almond milk

¼ cup (10 g) chopped chives

1 teaspoon ground cumin

½ teaspoon sea salt

Freshly ground pepper

CRUST

1 cup (100 g) almond flour

1 cup (120 g) chickpea flour

½ teaspoon baking powder

½ teaspoon sea salt

⅛ teaspoon freshly ground pepper

¼ cup (60 ml) plus 1 tablespoon extra virgin olive oil

1 to 2 tablespoons water

1 Preheat oven to 400°F (200°C) and grease a 10-inch skillet (or 9-inch tart pan); set aside.

2 Whisk together the filling ingredients and set aside.

3 In a large bowl, whisk together the flours, baking powder, salt, and pepper. Add the oil and use your hands to work into the flour until crumbly. Add 1 tablespoon of water and give the dough a squeeze; if it feels dry and doesn't stick together, drizzle in the remaining tablespoon of water until the dough sticks together. Turn the dough out into the skillet (or tart pan). Use your fingers to press into the bottom and sides of the pan. Bake the crust for 10 minutes; remove from the oven and turn the temperature down to 375°F (190°C). Add the egg filling and carefully place back in the oven; cook for 25 to 30 minutes, or until the eggs are firm and the center is set.

4 Let the quiche cool for 5 minutes and serve warm.

Early-Spring Veggie Bowl
with Warm Hummus Drizzle ⓥ

SERVES: 4 // **PREP TIME:** 30 MINUTES // **COOK TIME:** 45 MINUTES

Often when the seasons change our bodies need a break from the heaviness of winter meals. I find that eating lighter almost comes naturally. As spring arrives we're more inclined to grab a salad or prepare fresh vegetables in a lightly roasted form. This vegetable bowl is a good seasonal in-between—it combines a bit of roasted vegetables with some raw vegetables and a cooked grain. Using chickpea flour for hummus is a fast way to prepare the garlicky spread without the use of chickpeas in their whole, cooked form. You can prepare the hummus ahead of time and store in an airtight container for up to 1 week.

2 large yams (or sweet potatoes), cut into ½-inch cubes

1½ tablespoons plus 2 teaspoons extra virgin olive oil

½ teaspoon sumac

½ teaspoon plus a large pinch of sea salt

2 garlic cloves, minced, plus 1 clove, roughly chopped

1 teaspoon minced ginger

2 cups (60g) roughly chopped collard greens

¼ cup (30 g) plus 2 tablespoons chickpea flour

1¼ (300 ml) cups water

2 tablespoons tahini paste

1 tablespoon lemon juice

½ teaspoon ground cumin

Pinch of cayenne

1 cup (100 g) cooked brown rice

4 radishes, sliced paper-thin

1 teaspoon toasted black sesame seeds

½ cup (30 g) pea tendrils

❶ Preheat oven to 400°F (200°C) and line a rimmed baking sheet with parchment paper. In a large bowl, toss the potatoes with enough oil to coat, about 1½ tablespoons; add the sumac and a big pinch of salt, and mix. Turn out onto the baking sheet and roast for 35 to 40 minutes, until tender but not falling apart. Set aside.

❷ In a skillet, heat 2 teaspoons of oil over medium heat, add 2 minced cloves of garlic and the ginger, and stir. Cook for 30 seconds; then add the collards and cook until wilted. Remove from the heat and set aside.

❸ Heat a clean skillet over medium heat; add the flour and toast for 2 to 3 minutes, shaking the pan every few seconds to prevent burning, until the flour is toasted and nutty. Remove from the pan and place in a bowl to cool.

❹ In a small saucepan, whisk together the toasted flour and water until no lumps remain; turn the heat up to high and bring to a gentle boil. Reduce the heat to medium and bring to a simmer; stir occasionally until the mixture thickens, about 5 to 6 minutes. Remove from the heat and allow to cool for a few minutes.

❺ Combine the chickpea mixture, 1 clove of roughly chopped garlic, tahini paste, lemon juice, cumin, ½ teaspoon of salt, and cayenne in an upright blender; blend on high until you have a smooth consistency. Taste and adjust any seasonings. (Leftovers can be stored in a lidded jar in the refrigerator for up to 1 week. To warm the hummus, place in a saucepan over medium heat, adding water a little at a time until the hummus reaches the desired consistency.)

❻ Divide the potatoes, greens, rice, and radishes among four bowls. Drizzle with hummus and top with sesame seeds and pea tendrils.

Chickpea Noodles with Miso-Kale Pesto

SERVES: 4 AS A SIDE OR 2 AS A MEAL // **PREP TIME:** 1 HOUR // **COOK TIME:** 3 MINUTES

Gluten-free pasta is one of those things I buy very carefully at the grocery store; usually sticking to the one brand I know won't deliver mushy noodles. As I've learned throughout the years, store-bought gluten-free pasta can be finicky at times, so when I learned to make homemade pasta I was forever converted. The thought of hand making my pasta intimidated me, but after a few goes at it, it became a breeze.

PESTO

2 cups (60 g) kale
(preferably Lacinato)

1 cup (20 g) packed basil, plus whole
leaves for garnish

¼ cup (35 g) toasted pine nuts

2 garlic cloves, smashed
with the side of a knife

2 tablespoons gluten-free
mellow white miso

1 tablespoon lemon juice

¼ cup plus 2 tablespoons
extra virgin olive oil

NOODLES

1¾ cups (210 g) chickpea flour,
plus more for dusting

¼ cup (30 g) arrowroot powder

2 teaspoons psyllium husk powder

½ teaspoon sea salt

3 large eggs, at room temperature,
whisked

1 teaspoon water, or as needed

Handful of grated walnuts

❶ Make the pesto. Combine the kale, 1 cup of basil, pine nuts, garlic, miso, and lemon juice in a food processor; while the motor is running, drizzle in the oil until combined. Taste and adjust seasoning, adding more miso or lemon juice. Set aside.

❷ Make the noodles. In a large bowl, whisk together the flour, arrowroot, psyllium husk, and salt. Make a hole in the center of the flour mound and add the whisked eggs. Using a fork or your hands, slowly incorporate the flour into the whisked eggs until the dough is smooth; if the dough is dry, add water, a drop at a time, until the dough is smooth. If the dough is sticky and hard to work with, add more chickpea flour, a teaspoon at a time, until the dough is smooth.

❸ Knead the dough for approximately 10 minutes, or until completely smooth; it will look a bit like Play-Doh. Then shape the dough into a ball and place it on a chickpea-floured surface. Cover with a barely damp dish towel and let rest for 30 minutes.

❹ Line a baking sheet (or large cutting board) with parchment paper and sprinkle with chickpea flour; set aside.

❺ Place another piece of parchment on a clean work surface; generously sprinkle with more chickpea flour. Cut the dough into four even pieces, setting three pieces aside under your damp towel. Generously flour a rolling pin and roll the dough out into a rectangle with ⅛-inch thickness, lifting and turning the dough frequently to ensure it isn't sticking to the parchment.

❻ Trim the top and sides of the dough, and discard; slice the noodles ¼-inch wide and place on the floured baking sheet. Repeat with the remaining dough.

❼ Bring a large pot of salted water to a boil. Cook the noodles for about 2½ minutes; the pasta should be al dente—if not, cook for another 30 seconds, until cooked. Drain the noodles, reserving about ¼ cup of pasta water, and briefly run under cold water to stop the noodles from cooking.

❽ Place the pasta in a large serving bowl and toss with ½ cup of the pesto and a few tablespoons of the pasta water as needed and serve warm. Use the basil for garnish and sprinkle with grated walnuts.

Spring Onion and Lemongrass Stew with Cauliflower and Yams ⓥ

SERVES: 4 TO 6 // PREP TIME: 15 MINUTES // COOK TIME: 25 TO 30 MINUTES

I often find people swear off any form of soup the minute that spring arrives, but there is an abundance of vegetables that lend themselves to an entirely slurpable meal. Spring onions are one of them. While you can certainly sauté them, I find that their subtle, delicate, and somewhat understated taste is a perfect foundation for this soup. But the creaminess in this stew is where it's at. Toasted chickpea flour not only gives the stew proper substance but also provides it with nutty undertones that only add to the flavors here. Cauliflower and white yams keep the stew light and bright while also providing texture.

⅓ cup (40 g) chickpea flour

2 cups (480 ml) water

One 13.5-ounce (398 ml) can coconut milk

1 tablespoon coconut oil

1 bunch spring onions, bulbs and light green parts sliced thin

2 garlic cloves, minced

1 stalk lemongrass, trimmed and inner core chopped

One 1-inch piece of ginger, peeled and grated

1 teaspoon sea salt

½ teaspoon ground turmeric

1 large white yam, cut into 1-inch cubes*

2 cups (200 g) chopped cauliflower

1 cup (55 g) roughly chopped dandelion greens

1 tablespoon lime juice

Chopped chives

Chopped pistachios

❶ Toast the flour in a skillet over medium heat, stirring for 5 to 6 minutes, until lightly browned and fragrant. Remove from the heat and place in a large bowl; whisk in the water and milk until no lumps remain; set aside.

❷ Heat the oil in a large soup pot over medium heat. Once the pan is hot, add the sliced onions; cook until soft and translucent, about 5 minutes. Add the garlic, lemongrass, ginger, salt, and turmeric; stir and cook for about 40 seconds, until fragrant. Add the yam and cauliflower, stir and cook for 2 to 3 minutes. Add the flour and milk mixture. Raise the heat to high and bring to a boil. Cover and turn the heat down; simmer for 15 to 20 minutes, until the yam and cauliflower are just tender.

❸ Remove from the heat; stir in dandelion greens and lime juice. Serve with chopped chives and pistachios.

*Note: If white yams are not available to you, you can substitute sweet potatoes and prepare them as directed.

Grilled Harissa Cauliflower
with Quinoa Toss ⓥ

SERVES: 4 // **PREP TIME:** 1 TO 12 HOURS // **COOK TIME:** 15 MINUTES

This particular dish is a really easy weeknight meal—the quinoa toss, cauliflower, and marinade can be made simply ahead of time. The marinade's base is chickpea flour and harissa. The chickpea flour lends the marinade a bit of body, giving the grilled cauliflower a light batter. Harissa is a bold chili pepper paste, mostly composed of red peppers, hot peppers, coriander, caraway, and garlic. While you can certainly make your own, you can find premade harissa paste in the international aisle of many supermarkets.

1 head of cauliflower (about 840 g)

1 cup (120 g) chickpea flour

1 cup (240 ml) water

3 tablespoons extra virgin olive oil

2 tablespoons harissa paste

½ teaspoon apple cider vinegar

1 teaspoon sea salt, plus extra for the quinoa toss

1 tablespoon red wine vinegar

Freshly ground pepper

2 teaspoons maple syrup

2 cups (270 g) cooked quinoa

¼ cup (28 g) sliced almonds, toasted

¼ cup (30 g) dried currants

½ cup (90 g) green olives, pitted and sliced into quarters

½ cup (30 g) chopped parsley

❶ Rinse the cauliflower and remove any leaves. Cut the base off so the cauliflower head can stand up. Slice four cauliflower "steaks" and a few remaining pieces.

❷ In a large bowl, whisk together the flour, water, 1 tablespoon of oil, harissa, apple cider vinegar, and salt.

❸ Pour half the marinade in the bottom of a large baking dish or large platter; place the cut cauliflower in an even layer and pour the remaining marinade on top; use a pastry brush to distribute the marinade evenly. Cover with plastic wrap and refrigerate until ready to use, at least 1 hour, or up to 12 hours.

❹ Make the quinoa toss. In a small bowl, whisk together the red wine vinegar, a few pinches of salt, and pepper, to taste. Mix until the salt is dissolved. Whisk in 2 tablespoons of oil and the syrup, until the vinaigrette is emulsified. Set aside.

❺ In a large bowl, toss together the quinoa, almonds, currants, and olives. Drizzle in the vinaigrette and toss to combine; set aside.

❻ Heat a grill at medium-high heat and brush with oil. Place the cauliflower onto the grill; cook until light grill marks appear. Flip over and cook until golden brown and tender, but not mushy; about 5 minutes on each side. Serve warm over the quinoa toss. (If you don't have a grill, a lidded grill pan can be used in its place using the same technique.)

Lemony Panelle Sandwich
with Grilled Ramps and Balsamic Vinegar ⓥ

SERVES: 4 TO 6 // PREP TIME: 4 TO 12 HOURS // COOK TIME: 30 MINUTES

Panelle is a Sicilian street fritter made from chickpea flour and prepared between two pieces of bread to make a sandwich. You may have to plan this dish a bit in advance; the fritters have a resting period of about 4 hours to overnight. The chickpea flour is mixed with water, heated up, and thickened over the heat of a stove. It's then poured out onto a baking sheet in a thin layer, cooled in the refrigerator, sliced, and lightly fried. Many panelle sandwiches are served with ricotta cheese, but I prefer a slightly lighter version with zingy lemon juice, coarse salt, and lightly grilled ramps. Also known as wild leek, ramps are a sign of warmer weather to come. I generally use a thick, crusty bread (sandwich bread may prove too thin for this particular sandwich).

2 cups (480 ml) water

1 cup (120 g) chickpea flour

½ teaspoon sea salt

Freshly ground pepper

2 tablespoons plus 2 teaspoons extra virgin olive oil

2 bunches ramps, roots trimmed*

Coarse sea salt

1 loaf gluten-free focaccia or bread of choice

Balsamic vinegar, to taste

Lemon juice, to taste

❶ Lightly grease a large-rimmed baking sheet. Set aside.

❷ In a saucepan, whisk together the water, flour, salt, and pepper, to taste, until no lumps remain. Turn the heat to medium and whisk until the mixture thickens and starts pulling away from the sides of the pot, about 7 to 8 minutes. Quickly transfer to the prepared baking sheet; using a rubber spatula, evenly spread the mixture into a large rectangle with about ¼-inch thickness (this will vary depending on what size pan you use). Let sit at room temperature until cool, and then place in the refrigerator for at least 4 hours or overnight.

❸ Grill the ramps. Lightly brush a grill pan or grill with 1 to 2 teaspoons of oil, and turn the heat to medium-high. Once the pan is hot, add the ramps and sprinkle with coarse salt. Cook until each side has light grill marks, bulbs are soft, and greens are wilted. Place on a cutting board and let cool. Once cool, roughly chop and set aside.

❹ Remove the chickpea fritters from the refrigerator and slice into rectangles (the size can vary depending on the size of your bread). Use paper towels to blot any moisture, and heat a large skillet over medium heat; add 2 tablespoons of oil, enough oil to coat the bottom of the pan generously. Once the oil is hot and shimmering, add a few chickpea slices at a time and cook until golden brown, about 1 to 2 minutes on each side. Use a slotted spatula to transfer the fritters to a paper towel–lined plate. Repeat with the remaining fritters, adding more oil as needed.

❺ Toast your bread and drizzle each side with balsamic vinegar; stack about four chickpea fritters and divide the ramps among the sandwiches; top with a squeeze of lemon juice, and season with coarse salt and pepper.

*Note: If ramps are not available to you, spring onions or scallions will work as a replacement.

Asparagus Chickpea Frittata ⓥ

SERVES: 4 // **PREP TIME:** 15 MINUTES // **COOK TIME:** 40 TO 45 MINUTES

Vegans (and nonvegans) rejoice! Chickpea flour not only makes a wonderful egg substitute in frittatas, quiches, and scrambles, but also tastes incredibly delicious. Personally, I love eggs, but for those who don't or perhaps have family members or friends who can't eat eggs, chickpea flour can be your work-around. I was a little skeptical when I first tried a chickpea flour–based frittata, thinking that it couldn't possibly come close to the flavor or consistency of an egg. However, I was completely wrong. Not only does it stand up to egg-based frittatas, but I would say that I actually prefer it. When the batter is fully cooked it has a custard-like consistency, which is really hard to achieve with eggs without undercooking them. Paired with the fresh herbs, roasted asparagus, and mild leeks, this frittata tastes like it should have tons of cream and dairy in it, but it doesn't. My husband and I sometimes make this for a casual dinner or for a weekend breakfast. Leftovers can be refrigerated, heated back up, or eaten at room temperature. I even mash avocado on a piece of toast and put a piece of frittata on top, sandwich-style.

2 cups (480 ml) water

1 cup (120 g) chickpea flour

¼ cup (15 g) chopped mixed herbs (parsley, thyme, dill, and cilantro)

1 tablespoon plus 2 teaspoons extra virgin olive oil

1 teaspoon sea salt

½ teaspoon fennel seeds, crushed

Freshly ground pepper

1 large leek, trimmed, white and light green parts sliced thin

6 ounces (170 g) asparagus, woody ends trimmed and sliced in half lengthwise

1 teaspoon lemon juice

½ teaspoon Dijon mustard

❶ Preheat oven to 350°F (180°C) and grease an 8 x 8-inch square or round pan; set aside.

❷ In a large bowl, whisk together the water, flour, herbs, 1 tablespoon of oil, salt, fennel, and pepper, to taste, until no lumps remain. Set aside.

❸ Heat 1 teaspoon of oil in a skillet over medium heat. Once hot, add leeks; stir and cook for 3 to 4 minutes, until soft and translucent. Remove from the heat and mix into the batter.

❹ Toss the asparagus with the remaining 1 teaspoon of oil, lemon juice, and mustard; set aside.

❺ Add the batter to the prepared pan, and carefully transfer to the oven. Bake for 20 minutes; remove from the oven and layer the asparagus across the top of the frittata. Place back in the oven and bake for an additional 20 to 25 minutes, until solid and the asparagus is lightly browned. Let cool 30 minutes before slicing.

Lemon-Rhubarb Snacking Cake

MAKES: ONE 9 X 13-INCH RECTANGULAR CAKE // **SERVES:** 8 TO 10 // **PREP TIME:** 10 MINUTES
COOK TIME: 30 TO 35 MINUTES

I always loved the term "snacking cake"; it reminds me of my grandmother's generation, when taking part in a daily piece of cake was not just okay but the norm. I imagine eating this cake midafternoon, perhaps to break up a long workday or to come home to and enjoy with a cup of tea. This thin but hearty sheet cake has just the right amount of sweetness to balance out the rhubarb's tartness, while also incorporating hints of sweet lemon zest. The chickpea and almond flour provide the cake with a good amount of structure and flavor.

1 cup (120 g) chickpea flour

¾ cup (75 g) almond flour

¼ cup (30 g) arrowroot powder

2 teaspoons baking powder

1 teaspoon baking soda

¼ teaspoon sea salt

1 cup (144 g) coconut sugar

Zest from 1 lemon

2 large eggs

1 cup (252 g) applesauce

½ cup (120 ml) sunflower oil

1 teaspoon pure vanilla extract

1 teaspoon lemon extract

2 rhubarb stalks, ends trimmed and cut into ¼-inch pieces

❶ Preheat oven to 350°F (180°C) and grease a 9 x 13-inch pan.

❷ In a large bowl, whisk together the flours, arrowroot, baking powder, baking soda, and salt.

❸ In another large bowl, mix together the sugar and zest; use your fingers to massage the zest into the sugar, letting the zest's oils release. Continue to whisk in the eggs, applesauce, oil, and extracts. Slowly add the dry ingredients into the wet using a rubber spatula to mix; fold in the rhubarb, reserving a few pieces for the top of the cake.

❹ Pour the batter into the prepared pan; use a spatula to spread the batter evenly into the sides and corners of pan. Distribute the reserved rhubarb over the top. Bake for 30 to 35 minutes, until the sides have pulled away from the pan and the cake is lightly golden. Let cake cool completely before slicing.

❺ Cake can be stored at room temperature covered with parchment paper for up to 3 days.

Alfredo with Watercress and Chives ⓥ

SERVES: 4 // **PREP TIME:** 12 HOURS // **COOK TIME:** 20 MINUTES

Upon first discovering that chickpea flour can not only be used as a thickener in sauces but also made into a sauce all on its own, I was beyond excited for the possibilities, and the outcome of this sauce completely exceeded my expectations. Many, if not most, vegan cheese substitutes incorporate some type of nut that gives a cheese-like consistency when soaked and blended with water. However, I was always a little disappointed that my "cheese" sauces continually didn't have that gooey, cheesy texture. So when fooling around with a chickpea flour mix one day, I thought why not add it to the base of a vegan cheese sauce to give it that gooeyness I had longed for. After I added some flavorings, salt and pepper, and the like, I was amazed at the result: a cheese sauce tasting just the way I remember from my childhood. There are so many ways of incorporating this sauce into meals and dishes, whether it's over pasta, as a warm cheesy dip for vegetables, or poured over baked sweet potatoes or homemade french fries.

16 ounces (454 g) gluten-free and vegan pasta (or pasta of choice)

¼ cup (40 g) plus 1 tablespoon cashews, soaked overnight and drained

1 tablespoon extra virgin olive oil

1 tablespoon plus 1½ teaspoons nutritional yeast

2 teaspoons apple cider vinegar

1½ teaspoons lemon juice

2 garlic cloves, roughly chopped

½ teaspoon sea salt, plus more to taste

Freshly ground pepper

1 cup (240 ml) water

¼ cup (30 g) chickpea flour

2 tablespoons chopped chives, plus chive flowers for garnish

1 cup (34 g) packed watercress

Freshly ground nutmeg, to taste

❶ Begin cooking the pasta, according to instructions on the bag. While the pasta is cooking, make the sauce.

❷ Place the soaked cashews in an upright high-speed blender; add the oil, yeast, vinegar, lemon juice, garlic, salt, and pepper to taste; set aside.

❸ In a small saucepan, whisk together the water and flour, turn the heat to medium and continue to whisk for 6 to 7 minutes, until the mixture thickens to the consistency of a roux. Gently and carefully pour the mixture into the blender. Blend on high for 1 minute, until creamy and smooth. Taste and adjust any seasonings, if needed. Add 1 tablespoon of chives and blend on medium for about 30 seconds.

❹ In the last 30 seconds of cooking the pasta to al dente, add the watercress and cook until wilted. Drain the pasta and watercress and quickly rinse with cold water to stop them from cooking.

❺ Transfer the pasta and watercress to a serving bowl; pour the sauce over the pasta and mix. Taste and adjust salt, if needed. Serve hot with remaining 1 tablespoon of chives, chive flowers, and nutmeg.

Chickpea Polenta
with Sautéed Spring Vegetables ⓥ

SERVES: 4 // **PREP TIME:** 15 MINUTES // **COOK TIME:** 30 MINUTES

When I'm having a long day in the kitchen or working on freelance projects, I come home to make a really easy creamy polenta and sautéed vegetable bowl. While I make this all the time using various seasonal vegetables, my favorite time of year to make it is in the spring. I think there's something about the yellow polenta playing off the vibrant green vegetables that has me eating with my eyes before my taste buds get a chance. Chickpea flour is such a wonderful substitute for traditional polenta, since it's much easier to digest. It also has a really great texture and is faster to cook.

POLENTA

1 cup (120 g) chickpea flour

2 tablespoons nutritional yeast

¾ teaspoon sea salt

Freshly ground pepper

2 cups (480 ml) vegetable broth

1 cup (240 ml) water

SAUTÉED VEGETABLES

2 teaspoons extra virgin olive oil, plus extra for serving

4 ounces (105 g) ramps, roots trimmed, bulbs and leaves separated

2 garlic cloves, minced

6 ounces (189 g) broccoli rabe, thick stems trimmed, flowers reserved for garnish

2 tablespoons vegetable broth

Sea salt

Juice of 1 lemon

❶ Whisk together the flour, yeast, salt, and pepper, to taste; set aside.

❷ In a lidded saucepan, bring the vegetable broth and water to a boil. Remove the pan from the heat and whisk in the flour mixture; whisk constantly and place back onto the heat. Continue stirring for about 15 minutes, until the polenta has thickened; if you notice that the polenta has thickened too much, add more broth or water to thin out the consistency, and season accordingly.

❸ While the polenta is cooking, sauté the vegetables. Heat a skillet over medium heat; add the oil and sauté the ramp bulbs for 5 to 7 minutes, until soft and tender. Add the garlic and cook for 30 seconds, until fragrant. Then, add the broccoli rabe and vegetable broth; season with salt. Cook for another 5 minutes, until the broccoli is tender and the broth has reduced. Add the ramp leaves and sauté until wilted, about 1 minute. Remove the vegetables from the heat and set aside.

❹ Serve the polenta with the sautéed vegetables; top with a drizzle of olive oil, the lemon juice, and broccoli rabe flowers; season with salt and pepper.

Kalamata Chickpea Wrap
with Pickled Leeks and Microgreens

MAKES: FOUR 8-INCH WRAPS // **PREP TIME:** 20 MINUTES // **COOK TIME:** 10 TO 15 MINUTES

A chickpea mash just might be one of my favorite meals to put together in a flash. Most times I use canned chickpeas or leftover chickpeas cooked for another dish I made. Quickly pulsing the chickpeas in the food processor gives you a chunkier spread (as opposed to a hummus), which acts as a great binder when you want to pile high a sandwich or wrap. Oftentimes, I add whatever herbs I have laying around, and on occasion I add sun-dried tomatoes, but my favorite variation is adding briny Kalamata olives to the food processor so that you get flecks of olive in every bite. This wrap packs a lot of flavor and texture, from the olive-chickpea mash, to the lightly pickled leeks and the crunchy carrots and radishes. The wraps are quite pliable and stand up to folding taco-style or like a burrito.

CHICKPEA MASH

⅓ cup (80 ml) apple cider vinegar

1 teaspoon cane sugar

¼ teaspoon sea salt

1 leek, white and light green parts sliced thin

One 15-ounce (425 g) can chickpeas, drained and rinsed

2 tablespoons roughly chopped Kalamata olives

¼ cup (60 g) tahini paste

1 tablespoon plus 1½ teaspoons lemon juice

¾ teaspoon sea salt

⅛ teaspoon freshly ground pepper

WRAPS

1 cup (120 g) chickpea flour

1 cup (240 ml) water

1 large egg

½ teaspoon sea salt

Freshly ground pepper

1 teaspoon extra virgin olive oil

TOPPINGS

2 carrots, peeled into ribbons

2 radishes, sliced paper-thin

¼ cup (15 g) chopped cilantro

Microgreens

1 In a shallow bowl, whisk together the vinegar, sugar, and salt; add the leeks (if leeks are not completely submerged, add enough water to cover) and set aside for 10 minutes. Drain and rinse the leeks; pat dry and set aside.

2 Place the rinsed chickpeas and olives in a food processor fitted with a metal S blade; pulse four or five times until the beans and olives are chunky but not pureed. Transfer to a large mixing bowl; add the tahini, lemon juice, salt, and pepper; fold together until thoroughly combined. Taste and adjust any seasonings; set aside.

3 To make the wraps, whisk together the flour, water, egg, salt, and pepper, to taste.

4 Heat an 8- or 10-inch skillet over medium-high heat. Add a thin layer of oil, about 1 teaspoon, and swirl to cover the bottom of the pan. Once the oil is hot, pour about a ½ cup of batter onto the skillet, swirling around to make an 8-inch round. Cook for about 1 minute, until you see small bubbles forming all over the wrap; flip over and cook for another 45 seconds to 1 minute, until lightly golden. Remove and place on a plate; cover with a clean dish towel to keep warm. Repeat with the remaining batter, adding more cooking oil as needed.

5 Layer the wraps with chickpea mash; top with carrots, a few slices of radish, cilantro, pickled leeks, and a handful of microgreens.

Herbed Sweet Pea Pockets Ⓥ

MAKES: 8 POCKETS // **PREP TIME:** 40 MINUTES // **COOK TIME:** 15 TO 17 MINUTES

When I was growing up, Hot Pockets were all the rage, and my brother and I had a moment where all we ate were pizza Hot Pockets. However, eventually we came to the realization that this phase wasn't the best for us. But the pocket is still a relevant vessel for so many things that don't include oozy cheese and red sauce. Enter: the vegetable pocket!

These pockets are filled with chunky potato, lightly sautéed leeks, and freshly shelled peas. The dough comes together quite easily and can be used any time of year for seasonal variations.

FILLING

1 large potato, cut into ½-inch cubes (about 1 cup / 215 g)

1 tablespoon extra virgin olive oil

½ cup (60 g) leeks, cleaned and white and light green parts thinly sliced

2 garlic cloves, minced

½ cup (70 g) freshly shelled English peas

¼ cup (15 g) packed chopped mixed herbs (basil, thyme, chives, parsley)

½ teaspoon chili powder

Juice of ½ lime

Sea salt and freshly ground pepper

DOUGH

1 cup (120 g) chickpea flour

1 cup (110 g) sorghum flour, plus more for dusting

1 teaspoon psyllium husk powder

1 teaspoon sea salt

2 tablespoons plus 1½ teaspoons extra virgin olive oil

½ cup (120 ml) water

❶ Bring a pot of water to a boil. Add the potato, turn the heat to low, and cover. Cook for 10 to 15 minutes, until a knife can easily pierce the potato. Drain the potato and place in a large bowl; mash with a potato masher until chunky. Set aside.

❷ Coat the bottom of a skillet with enough oil to cover, about 1 tablespoon, and heat over medium. Once the pan is hot, add the leeks and cook for 3 to 4 minutes, until soft. Add garlic and cook for another 30 to 40 seconds, until fragrant. Add the peas, herbs, chili powder, and lime juice; cook for another 5 minutes, until the peas are tender and the lime juice has reduced. Remove from the heat and fold into the mashed potatoes; season with salt and pepper, to taste. Set aside while you make the dough.

❸ In a large mixing bowl, whisk together the flours, psyllium husk, and salt. Drizzle in the oil and use your hands to distribute, then add ¼ cup of water, mixing it in with your hands. Knead the dough until smooth, about 3 minutes; cover with a damp cloth and let rest for 10 minutes. Keep adding water if needed. (The amount of water needed varies depending on altitude, humidity, and temperature. Add the remaining ¼ cup a little at a time until the dough is smooth.)

❹ Preheat oven to 400°F (200°C) and line a baking sheet with parchment paper.

❺ Prepare a flat work surface with a large piece of parchment paper and divide the dough into eight equal pieces. Roll out one piece into a flat circle. Fill one side of the dough with roughly 2 tablespoons of filling. Fold the other side up and over the filling, and pinch the edges to seal. Repeat with the remaining dough and filling. Place on the prepared baking sheet.

❻ Bake for 16 to 18 minutes, until golden brown. Let cool 5 minutes before serving. Pockets are best served the day of, but can be refrigerated for up to 2 days.

Vanilla Bean Lavender Cupcakes

MAKES: 12 CUPCAKES // **PREP TIME:** 15 MINUTES // **COOK TIME:** 12 TO 15 MINUTES

Lavender is something I always incorporate into a Mother's Day treat, whether it's sneaking a bit of the buds into a whipping cream or infusing it into a syrup, it's a favorite springtime flavor that is often underutilized in the kitchen. Here is a basic yellow cupcake that incorporates a good amount of chickpea flour, giving this dessert not only a nutritional sturdiness but also a textural one. What's wonderful about baking with a high-protein flour is that it doesn't give your blood sugar a spike and leave you depleted. Instead, you're able to enjoy a sweet treat without worrying about the consequences.

CUPCAKES

¼ cup (60 ml) sunflower oil

⅔ cup (150 g) cane sugar

2 large eggs

½ cup (120 ml) almond milk

1 vanilla bean, scraped (if you don't have a vanilla bean, use 1 teaspoon pure vanilla extract in its place)

1 cup (120 g) chickpea flour

½ cup (70 g) brown rice flour

2 tablespoons arrowroot powder

2 teaspoons baking powder

½ teaspoon sea salt

LAVENDER CREAM

Two 13.5-ounce (398 ml each) cans coconut milk, refrigerated overnight

3 tablespoons maple syrup

1 tablespoon coconut oil, melted and cooled

1 teaspoon pure vanilla extract

2 teaspoons dried organic lavender, plus more for garnish

① Preheat oven to 350°F (180°C) and line a twelve-cup muffin pan with liners; set aside.

② Using an electric mixer, beat together the sunflower oil and sugar on medium speed until the sugar is dissolved, about 1 minute; mix in the eggs, almond milk, and vanilla. Set aside.

③ In a separate bowl, whisk together the flours, arrowroot, baking powder, and salt. Using a rubber spatula, add the dry ingredients to the wet until combined.

④ Divide the batter evenly among the muffin molds and bake for 18 to 20 minutes, until a cake tester inserted into the center of a cupcake comes out clean.

⑤ Remove from the oven and allow the cupcakes to cool completely, at least 2 hours.

⑥ While the cupcakes are cooling, make the lavender cream. Remove the coconut milk from refrigerator, turn the cans upside down, and remove the bottoms of the cans. Carefully drain off the coconut water (reserve for smoothies or other uses), and scoop the solidified coconut cream out into a mixing bowl. With an electric mixer, beat together the coconut cream, syrup, coconut oil, and vanilla, until smooth and creamy. Fold in the dried lavender. Cover the bowl with plastic wrap and place in the refrigerator until ready to use.

⑦ Frost the cupcakes with the lavender cream. Sprinkle the tops with extra lavender for decoration.

Strawberry Tart
with Cardamom-Coconut Cream ⓥ

MAKES: ONE 8-INCH ROUND TART // **SERVES:** 8 // **PREP TIME:** 15 MINUTES // **COOK TIME:** 1 HOUR

This is a perfect recipe to make when you have a basket of radiant farm-fresh strawberries that are sweet, juicy, and at their peak. Often you can tell a ripe strawberry by its color and smell, but sometimes the best way to find out is to give one a taste before purchasing just to make sure you're going home with the sweetest bunch you can find. This tart is really all about simplicity—each component sings beautifully on its own, but when combined, this tart will really impress.

TART CRUST

¾ cup (79 g) gluten-free old-fashioned rolled oats

½ cup (60 g) chickpea flour

¼ cup (35 g) almonds

Pinch of sea salt

3 tablespoons coconut oil, melted

2 tablespoons maple syrup

FILLING

One 13.5-ounce (398 ml) can coconut milk, refrigerated overnight

1 tablespoon maple syrup

1 teaspoon pure vanilla extract

½ teaspoon ground cardamom

2 pints strawberries, sliced in half or, if large, in quarters

❶ Preheat oven to 350°F (180°C). Grease a tart pan and set aside.

❷ In a food processor fitted with a metal S blade, pulse together the oats, flour, almonds, and salt until thoroughly ground, about 30 seconds. Transfer to a bowl and pour in melted oil and syrup; use a fork or your hands to mix together thoroughly until combined. Turn the dough out into the tart pan, and use your fingers to press the dough evenly into the bottoms and sides of the pan. Bake for 28 to 30 minutes, until the crust is golden brown. Set aside and let cool completely.

❸ Remove milk from the refrigerator and place upside down. Open the can from the bottom and pour coconut water out (reserve if desired); scoop coconut cream from the bottom of the can and place in a bowl. If the cream is very stiff, let it rest for 10 minutes.

❹ Using an electric mixer, beat together coconut cream, syrup, vanilla, and cardamom until creamy. Use a spatula to scrape cream evenly into cooled tart shell; arrange strawberries in concentric circles starting from the inside and working out. Pile extra strawberry halves in the center.

❺ Tart is best eaten the day of but can be stored in the refrigerator for 2 days.

Cherry Dutch Baby

MAKES: ONE 10-INCH DUTCH BABY PANCAKE // **SERVES:** 4 // **PREP TIME:** 10 MINUTES
COOK TIME: 18 TO 20 MINUTES

A Dutch baby is something that had eluded my kitchen until I was lucky enough to eat one a few years ago. While the one I tasted wasn't exactly the same as a Dutch baby, or German pancake, the idea of a very large, almost soufflé- and omelet-like sweet pancake was enough to sway me to give it a try in my own kitchen. They're unbelievably easy to make and impressive to serve for brunch or even as dessert. Cherry season is short here in New York, so I try to use them up in just about everything from syrups to salads and in baked breakfasts like this one. You won't find this pancake to be too sweet—it's very subtle—but for a sweeter flavor, shower the top with a bit of confectioners' sugar.

½ cup (60 g) chickpea flour

2 tablespoons cane sugar

Zest from ½ lemon

¼ teaspoon sea salt

3 large eggs

½ cup (120 ml) almond milk

1 teaspoon pure vanilla extract

2 tablespoons coconut oil, melted

1 heaping cup (185 g) cherries, pitted and halved

Confectioners' sugar, to taste

❶ Preheat oven to 425°F (220°C).

❷ In a blender, combine the flour, sugar, zest, salt, eggs, milk, and vanilla; blend on high for 30 seconds, until thoroughly combined. Set aside.

❸ Heat an oven-safe 10-inch skillet over medium heat. Splash with a drop of water: if the water sizzles and evaporates, the pan is ready. Add the oil and cherries; cook, stirring every few minutes, until the cherries are soft, about 5 minutes. Turn the heat off.

❹ Give the batter another whiz in the blender, then pour the batter into the pan with the cherries; carefully transfer to the oven.

❺ Bake for 18 to 20 minutes, until puffed and lightly browned around edges.

❻ Top with a dusting of confectioners' sugar and serve hot.

Baby Chickpea Quiches
with New Potatoes and Chard ⓥ

MAKES: 24 MINI QUICHES // **SERVES:** 8 TO 12 // **PREP TIME:** 25 MINUTES // **COOK TIME:** 20 TO 22 MINUTES

I often have a hard time deciding what kind of vegetables to put in my quiche, especially at this time of year when my refrigerator is packed with fresh market produce. A quiche is a great way to use up some of your CSA goods or the abundance of vegetables purchased at the farmers' market. Potatoes are at their height during the summer and many times require less cooking because they're so fresh and tender, which is why I love using them here. They add a subtle texture with the wilted chard. If you can't find fingerling or new potatoes, any small potatoes will do. These mini quiches are great to serve for a brunch or even to make on a Sunday to have leftovers for breakfast, dinner, or lunch. If you're not a fan of cumin, use ½ teaspoon or leave it out entirely.

10 ounces (300 g) fingerling or new potatoes

2 tablespoons plus 2 teaspoons extra virgin olive oil

1 small onion, finely diced

2 garlic cloves, minced

4 large Swiss chard leaves, chopped

Few pinches of coarse sea salt

2¼ (270 g) cups chickpea flour

1 tablespoon nutritional yeast

2 teaspoons sea salt

1 teaspoon ground cumin

⅛ teaspoon freshly ground pepper

3 cups (720 ml) water

1 teaspoon gluten-free tamari

2 tablespoons chopped dill, plus more for garnish

❶ Preheat oven to 400°F (200°C) and grease two 12-cup muffin pans; set aside.

❷ In a large pot filled with water, bring the potatoes to a boil, cover, and turn the heat to low so there's a rolling simmer. Cook the potatoes until knife-tender, about 10 to 15 minutes. Drain and let cool and then slice the potatoes into ¼-inch pieces; set aside.

❸ Heat 2 teaspoons oil in a skillet; once hot, add the onion and sauté until soft and translucent, about 3 minutes. Add the garlic and stir, cook for 30 seconds, until fragrant. Add the chard and a few pinches of coarse salt; cook until wilted, 30 to 45 seconds. Turn the heat off and set aside.

❹ In a large bowl, whisk together the flour, yeast, salt, cumin, and pepper. Drizzle in the water while whisking, until no lumps remain; add 2 tablespoons of oil and the tamari; whisk until mixed. Stir in the sautéed vegetables, potatoes, and dill. Divide the batter among the twenty-four muffin molds and bake for 20 to 22 minutes, rotating halfway through, until lightly browned. Allow to cool for 10 minutes; serve warm with extra dill.

Stuffed Squash Blossoms
with Macadamia Ricotta Ⓥ

MAKES: 10 TO 12 BLOSSOMS // **SERVES:** 4 TO 6 // **PREP TIME:** 12 HOURS // **COOK TIME:** 25 MINUTES

If there's one thing I truly look forward to frying each summer it's squash blossoms. The first time I had a stuffed squash blossom was at a restaurant on Martha's Vineyard called Ice House. They were very much an eat-from-the-land restaurant that really respected not only where the food they were serving came from but also how they prepared it. It was a lightly fried blossom filled with a warm and subtle goat cheese that tasted both light and airy but substantial at the same time. While I've attempted to re-create that preparation, my diet has changed a lot since then. Here, I prepare the squash blossoms by stuffing them with vegan cheese and using various flours for the batter—all with wonderful results.

RICOTTA

½ cup (63 g) raw macadamia nuts, soaked overnight or at least 6 hours

4 to 5 tablespoons water

1 tablespoon nutritional yeast

1½ teaspoons apple cider vinegar

1 teaspoon lemon juice

1 teaspoon gluten-free mellow white miso

1 garlic clove, minced

¼ teaspoon sea salt

2 tablespoons chopped parsley

BLOSSOMS

10 to 12 squash blossoms

1 cup (120 g) chickpea flour

Big pinch of coarse sea salt

1 cup ice water

½ cup (120 ml) sunflower oil

❶ Drain and rinse the macadamia nuts; place in a high-speed blender (or food processor, although the consistency won't be as smooth) with 4 tablespoons of water, yeast, vinegar, lemon juice, miso, garlic, and salt. Blend on high, stopping to scrape down the sides as needed, until you have a smooth, creamy consistency. You may find that adding the additional tablespoon of water is necessary to achieve a creamy texture. Transfer the filling to a bowl, mix in the parsley, and cover with plastic wrap; place in the refrigerator until ready to use.

❷ When ready to make the stuffed blossoms, remove the macadamia ricotta from the refrigerator. Using a paring knife, make a slit on the side of each blossom. If there is a stamen (the center of the flower covered with pollen), carefully remove it with a knife and discard. Using a small spoon, stuff each blossom with the macadamia filling; twist the end of each blossom to close. Set aside.

❸ To make the batter, whisk together the flour and salt, then whisk in the water; set aside.

❹ Line a large plate or platter with a layer of paper towels; set aside. Heat ¼-inch of oil in a skillet over medium heat, until shimmering. In batches, dunk the squash blossoms into the batter; use a fork to lift them out, grabbing them gently by the stem and letting any excess batter drip off. Fry for 45 seconds to 1 minute, until golden brown; flip over and fry the other side for another 30 to 45 seconds, until golden and crisp. Remove blossoms and transfer to prepared platter to remove excess oil. Serve hot.

Chickpea-Halloumi Salad
with Crispy Quinoa Ⓥ

SERVES: 4 AS A SIDE OR 2 AS A MEAL // **PREP TIME:** 12 HOURS // **COOK TIME:** 45 MINUTES

Halloumi is a Greek cheese that works very well for grilling and frying. It's quite salty, however, though not as salty as Feta cheese, and has a gooey consistency when heated. I use the word "halloumi" quite loosely here, since the consistency is different than traditional halloumi, but the crisp outside and gooey inside is quite similar. The chickpea halloumi is prepared the night before (it needs ample time to solidify in the refrigerator) and then grilled the next day. I love eating it plain, adding it to grain or green salads, or preparing it along with a traditional meze platter. The halloumi can also be prepared in a grill pan on the stove or panfried with a light layer of oil.

HALLOUMI

1 cup (120 g) chickpea flour

2 tablespoons nutritional yeast

2½ teaspoons sea salt

½ teaspoon onion powder

2 cups (480 ml) water

1 teaspoon apple cider vinegar

VINAIGRETTE

3 tablespoons lemon juice

1½ teaspoons quality Dijon mustard (preferably Maille)

Sea salt and freshly ground pepper

¼ cup (60 ml) extra virgin olive oil

1 teaspoon maple syrup

SALAD

½ cup (74 g) cooked quinoa

2 teaspoons extra virgin olive oil

1 cup (19 g) baby arugula

2 cups (28 g) mesclun mix

½ cucumber, or 1 small cucumber, cut into ⅛-inch slices

2 tablespoons toasted sunflower seeds

Leaves from 2 mint sprigs, roughly chopped

¼ cup (15 g) herb flowers (optional)

1 The day before making the salad, prepare the halloumi. Lightly grease a 9 x 13-inch pan with oil; set aside. In a small saucepan, whisk together the flour, yeast, salt, and onion powder; whisk in the water and vinegar until no lumps remain.

2 Turn the heat to medium and continue to whisk the mixture every few seconds to prevent scorching. Keep whisking until the mixture has thickened to a pudding-like consistency, about 7 to 8 minutes. Quickly remove the mixture from the heat and pour into the prepared pan; use a rubber spatula to spread the mixture evenly into the pan. Let the mixture come to room temperature, then store uncovered in the refrigerator.

3 While the chickpea mixture is cooling, make the vinaigrette. Whisk together the lemon juice, mustard, and salt and pepper, to taste, until the salt is dissolved; whisk in the oil and syrup until emulsified. Set aside.

4 The day of making the salad, remove the chickpea halloumi from the refrigerator. Slice in half lengthwise and then into eight pieces. Place the pieces between two paper towels to remove any excess moisture; set aside.

5 To crisp the quinoa, heat 2 teaspoons oil over medium heat in a skillet. Fry the quinoa until crisp and golden; you will hear the quinoa pop when it's ready, about 8 to 10 minutes. Set aside.

6 Heat a grill over medium-high heat and oil liberally; brush the halloumi with oil and grill until there are light grill marks and the halloumi is hot, about 2 minutes on each side.

7 Toss the quinoa, arugula, mesclun, cucumber, seeds, and mint with 2 to 3 tablespoons of the vinaigrette; top with hot halloumi and herb flowers and serve.

Chickpea Pizza with Asparagus and Pea Shoot Tangle ⓥ

MAKES: TWO 11-INCH PIZZAS // **PREP TIME:** 1 HOUR 30 MINUTES // **COOK TIME:** 10 TO 15 MINUTES

Gluten-free pizza dough is really hard to come by, especially when you're looking for one that doesn't have a long list of hard-to-digest gums and starches. When I first started making my own pizza dough, I was super surprised to find out how easy it was and was even happier that I could make an eggless one for when my vegan family members and friends come over. The chickpea flour adds a bit of sturdiness and substance, not to mention a bit of protein as well, making this pizza ideal for a wholesome meal. While you can add whatever toppings you please, I love going for more of a salad vibe, especially when there's tons of delicious and beautiful spring produce at every turn.

DOUGH*

1¼ cups warm water (105°–115°F)

1 teaspoon natural cane sugar (or 1 teaspoon raw honey)

1 packet instant yeast (approximately 2¼ teaspoons)

1 cup (140 g) brown rice flour

1 cup (120 g) chickpea flour

½ cup (55 g) sorghum flour, plus more for dusting

½ cup (60 g) arrowroot powder

2 teaspoons psyllium husk powder

1½ teaspoons sea salt

2 tablespoons extra virgin olive oil

TOPPINGS

1 bunch asparagus (456 g), peeled into ribbons

2 tablespoons capers

1 tablespoon extra virgin olive oil

1½ teaspoons lemon juice

Sea salt and freshly ground pepper

2 cups (112 g) pea shoots

8 ounces garlic hummus, or hummus of choice

❶ In a mixing bowl, whisk together the water and cane sugar until dissolved; sprinkle in the yeast and let the yeast proof for about 10 minutes, until the surface is foamy and bubbly; if yeast does not proof, start over with more yeast.

❷ In a large bowl, whisk together the flours, arrowroot, psyllium husk, and salt. Make a well in the center of the bowl and add the yeast mixture and oil. Using a dough hook on an electric mixer or a paddle attachment on a stand mixer, mix the dough until smooth. Dough should be able to hold its form but be sticky to the touch. If the dough is too sticky and not able to hold its form, add more chickpea flour 1 tablespoon at a time until the dough is firmer. Cover the dough in the bowl loosely with plastic wrap and allow dough to rise in a warm place for 30 to 45 minutes, until roughly doubled in size.

❸ Place a wire rack at the lowest position in your oven, place a baking stone or baking sheet on it, and preheat oven to 500°F (260°C).

❹ Line two baking sheets with parchment paper and lightly dust them with sorghum flour. Using a dough scraper, divide the dough into two even pieces; gently form each piece of dough into a ball. Place a piece of dough on each prepared piece of parchment; dust the dough with a light coating of flour and press it into an 11-inch round, working your fingers from the inside of the dough to the outside until the crust is about ¼-inch thick, dusting with more flour as needed.

❺ Cover the dough loosely with plastic wrap and allow the dough to rise once more for 15 to 20 minutes; dough should puff up slightly and be springy to the touch.

❻ While the dough is rising again, prepare the toppings. In a large bowl, combine the asparagus, capers, 2 teaspoons of oil, and 1 teaspoon of lemon juice; season with salt and pepper. In a separate bowl, combine the pea shoots with the remaining 1 teaspoon of oil and ½ teaspoon lemon juice; season with salt and pepper; set aside.

⓻ Use a pizza peel or cookie sheet to gently slide one piece of parchment with the dough onto the baking stone and bake for 5 minutes, until the dough is slightly golden and a bit stiff. Use the peel to slide the dough out of the oven, and spread half the hummus over top of the pizza; then distribute half the asparagus and capers over the hummus; place back in the oven and bake until the edges are lightly browned and crisp and asparagus is lightly charred in places, about 8 to 10 minutes.

⓼ Remove the pizza from the oven and top with pea shoots. Let the pizza rest for 5 minutes to let the pea shoots wilt a bit. Serve warm or at room temperature.

⓽ Repeat with remaining dough and toppings.

*Note: Pizza dough can be stored in the freezer for up to 1 month. To thaw, remove from the freezer the morning of, or at least 5 hours before cooking, and allow the dough to come to room temperature. If not using the dough right away, store in the refrigerator until ready. Prepare the dough as directed.

Grilled Zucchini Tacos
with Chickpea-Chipotle Crema ⓥ

SERVES: 4 TO 6 // **PREP TIME:** 12 HOURS // **COOK TIME:** 15 MINUTES

Tacos make the perfect vessel for just about anything regardless of the season. But for the summer, I love grilled vegetable tacos more than anything; the light char makes them that much more delicious! These summer tacos are filled with a bit of hearty quinoa, spiced and grilled zucchini, pumpkin seeds for crunch, and a healthy dose of chipotle chickpea crema.

CREMA

½ cup (80 g) raw cashews, soaked overnight and drained

1 garlic clove, roughly chopped

1 shallot, roughly chopped

1 tablespoon lime juice

½ teaspoon chipotle powder

½ teaspoon sea salt

1 cup (240 ml) water

¼ cup (30 g) chickpea flour

TACO FILLING

1 cup (240 ml) water

½ cup (95 g) quinoa

Sea salt

2 tablespoons extra virgin olive oil

1 jalapeño, seeded and roughly chopped

½ medium red onion, diced

2 tablespoons toasted pumpkin seeds

1 tablespoon chopped cilantro, plus more for garnish

1 tablespoon lime juice

Freshly ground pepper

2 medium zucchinis

½ teaspoon ground cumin

¼ teaspoon chili powder

Pinch of cayenne (optional)

6 corn tortillas, toasted

Sesame seeds, to taste

① In a high-speed blender, blend the cashews, garlic, shallot, lime juice, chipotle powder, and salt; set aside. In a saucepan, whisk together the water and flour until no lumps remain; turn the heat to medium and whisk every few seconds to prevent scorching. Continue whisking for another 1½ to 2 minutes, until the mixture is thickened (similar to a pudding). Remove from the heat and pour into the blender. Blend on high for 1 minute, until smooth and creamy. Taste and adjust the seasoning, if needed. Transfer to a bowl until cool, then refrigerate. When ready to use, whisk in water ½ teaspoon at a time until you reach desired consistency; adjust any seasonings. (Crema can be made up to 2 to 3 days in advance and stored in the refrigerator.)

② Combine the water, quinoa, and a pinch of salt in a saucepan and bring to a boil, cover the pan, and turn the heat to low. Simmer for 12 to 15 minutes, or until all the water is absorbed. Place the quinoa in a large bowl and set aside.

③ Heat 2 to 3 teaspoons of oil (enough to coat the bottom) in a skillet over medium. Once the pan is hot, add the jalapeño and onion; stir and cook until both are soft, about 5 minutes. Remove from the heat and toss in with the quinoa; mix in the toasted pumpkin seeds, cilantro, and lime juice, season with salt and pepper, and set aside.

④ Heat a grill to medium heat (roughly 350°F/180°C to 400°F/200°C). While the grill is heating, slice off top of each zucchini, then cut in half crosswise; slice each half into quarters, giving you sixteen pieces total. Place in a bowl and toss with the remaining 1 tablespoon of oil, cumin, chili powder, and cayenne (if using), until combined; set aside.

⑤ Brush the grill with oil; grill the zucchini until lightly charred and tender, about 2 minutes on either side. Depending on the size of your tortillas, cut the zucchini into thirds or in half.

⑥ Top the toasted tortillas with the chipotle crema, quinoa, zucchini, chopped cilantro, and sesame seeds, and drizzle a bit more crema on top.

Nutty Oat Ice-Cream Sandwiches

MAKES: 12 SANDWICHES // **PREP TIME:** 30 MINUTES // **COOK TIME:** 12 TO 14 MINUTES

Ice-cream sandwiches take us all back to a time when we were kids playing outside with friends. At a certain moment, we would hear the sound of the ice-cream truck from a distance, and then run inside to scrounge up just enough change to buy our favorite frozen snack. Mine was always vanilla ice cream, sandwiched between two soft chocolate cookies, because ice-cream sandwiches combined two beloved sweets: cookies and ice cream. This riff on the original incorporates a lovely oat-textured cookie, vanilla ice cream, and a salt-licked nutty crumble that coats the exposed ice cream.

1½ cups (157 g) gluten-free old-fashioned rolled oats

1 cup (120 g) chickpea flour

½ cup (70 g) brown rice flour

1½ teaspoons baking powder

½ teaspoon baking soda

½ teaspoon sea salt

1½ cups (216 g) coconut sugar

½ cup (120 ml) coconut oil, melted but cool

2 large eggs

¼ cup (60 ml) almond milk

1 teaspoon pure vanilla extract

2 pints dairy-free vanilla ice cream (or ice cream of choice)

⅓ cup (40 g) salted peanuts, crushed

1 Preheat oven to 350°F (180°F) and line two cookie sheets with parchment paper; set aside.

2 In a large bowl, whisk together the oats, flours, baking powder, baking soda, and salt; set aside.

3 In a separate bowl, whisk together the sugar and oil, add the eggs, milk, and vanilla, and whisk until incorporated. Using a rubber spatula, add the dry mix into the wet mix, and fold until thoroughly incorporated. Cover the dough with plastic wrap and refrigerate for 20 minutes.

4 Using a tablespoon measure, scoop the dough and form a ball with your hands. Place on the prepared baking sheet and flatten with your palm. Repeat with remaining dough. Bake for 16 to 18 minutes, rotating halfway through, until lightly golden. Let cool completely.

5 Remove the ice cream from the freezer and allow it to soften a bit before scooping, about 5 to 10 minutes. Place the crushed peanuts in a shallow dish or plate. Scoop desired amount of ice cream between two cookies and roll the sides of the exposed ice cream into the ground peanuts and place on a platter or baking sheet; transfer to the freezer while you assemble the remaining sandwiches. Remove from the freezer and serve immediately. Sandwiches can be stored in the freezer in an airtight container for up to 1 week.

Strawberry S'mores ⓥ

MAKES: 8 S'MORES // **PREP TIME:** 40 MINUTES // **COOK TIME:** 15 TO 18 MINUTES

I'm quite sure s'mores bring back all sorts of childhood nostalgia for us all: thoughts of gooey toasted marshmallows, sticky hands, and bits of melted chocolate in the crease of your lips. I wanted to revisit this old classic and give it a bit of a makeover, one with homemade graham crackers and fresh, juicy strawberries. The hint of berries has a way of transforming this treat into something that's a little less decadent and sweet.

1 cup (120 g) chickpea flour

¾ cup (105 g) brown rice flour, plus more for dusting

¼ cup (30 g) arrowroot powder

¼ cup (36 g) coconut sugar

1 teaspoon baking powder

¾ teaspoon ground cinnamon

¼ teaspoon sea salt

¼ cup plus 1 tablespoon almond milk

3 tablespoons extra virgin olive oil

2 tablespoons plus 1½ teaspoons maple syrup

8 to 16 vegan marshmallows (or marshmallows of choice)

4 ounces (113 g) chocolate (60 to 70 percent cacao), broken into 8 squares

8 ripe strawberries

1. Preheat oven to 350°F (180°C).

2. Place the flours, arrowroot, sugar, baking powder, cinnamon, and salt in a food processor fitted with a metal S blade. Pulse a few times to combine ingredients. With the motor running, drizzle in the milk, oil, and syrup until the dough forms a uniform ball. Stop the motor and remove the top, then pinch the dough between your fingers. It should be moist and sticky; if your dough is crumbly, drizzle in more milk ½ teaspoon at a time, testing dough each time you add more liquid.

3. Prepare a flat work surface and line it with parchment paper, roughly 15 x 13 inches. Dust the paper, rolling pin, and dough with brown rice flour. Roll the dough into a square with a ⅛-inch thickness; trim the edges—you should have a roughly 12 x 13-inch square of dough. Slide a baking sheet underneath the parchment and dough.

4. Using a sharp knife or pizza cutter, score the dough lengthwise in quarters and then score in quarters widthwise, giving you sixteen squares. Using a fork, poke decorative holes in the tops of the dough.

5. Bake the crackers for 15 to 18 minutes, until lightly browned and golden. Let the crackers cool completely before breaking apart and assembling the s'mores.

6. Heat a grill to a moderate heat (alternatively, you can toast marshmallows over the heat of a stove if you don't have access to a grill). Thread the marshmallows on skewers and toast, turning to heat all sides, until golden and mushy.

7. Place one piece of chocolate on one graham cracker and lay 1 or 2 marshmallows on top; place a strawberry on top of the other graham cracker and use a fork to crush it. Sandwich the crackers together and allow the s'mores to sit and melt the chocolate a bit. Repeat with the remaining crackers and serve immediately.

Summer Months

Summer is a season that's leisurely, but alive and active; that's sweltering, but refreshing; and that uses and celebrates all the senses. If there were ever a season to savor, summer would surely be it. Its abundance is only available for so long before we part with it once again. I think because of its evanescence and the nostalgia it holds for us all, it's perhaps the most admired season. I tried to capture the feeling of summer that is evoked with enjoying a big beautiful salad, cooking skewers on the grill, eating ice-cream sandwiches that melt faster than you're able to eat them—all while using what's most fresh and at its peak each month. Tomatoes are that much more vibrant and juicier in August, figs are their most ripe and sweet in September, and throughout, summer corn is so tender that you could eat it right off the cob without having to cook it. Those are the thoughts and flavors that inspire each of these summer recipes.

Lemon-Blueberry Coffee Cake

MAKES: ONE 8-INCH ROUND COFFEE CAKE // **SERVES:** 8 // **PREP TIME:** 20 MINUTES
COOK TIME: 50 TO 55 MINUTES

This coffee cake is somewhat of a departure from the overly sweet, decadent coffee cakes we all know from bakeries. It has a light and crumbly lemon zest streusel with a cake that has a velvety texture and a hint of cinnamon, giving a nod to coffee cakes past. The blueberries add a fruity element not commonly found in a coffee cake, breaking up the cake's texture and offering a subtle burst of fresh juiciness. While I call for an 8-inch springform pan for easy removal, you can certainly use an 8-inch cake pan with 2-inch sides.

STREUSEL

½ cup (55 g) sorghum flour
¼ cup slivered almonds
2 teaspoons lemon zest
¼ teaspoon ground cinnamon
Pinch of sea salt
2 tablespoons coconut oil, melted
1 tablespoon maple syrup

CAKE

½ cup (120 ml) coconut milk
1½ teaspoons apple cider vinegar
1 cup (120 g) chickpea flour
½ cup (70 g) brown rice flour
1 teaspoon baking powder
½ teaspoon baking soda
1 teaspoon ground cinnamon
½ teaspoon sea salt
2 large eggs
¼ cup (60 ml) sunflower oil
⅔ cup (96 g) coconut sugar
½ teaspoon lemon extract
½ teaspoon pure vanilla extract
½ pint (150 g) blueberries

1 Preheat oven to 350°F (180°C) and grease an 8-inch springform pan; set aside.

2 For the streusel, whisk together the sorghum flour, almonds, lemon zest, cinnamon, and salt; drizzle in the coconut oil and syrup; toss together with a fork until wet and clumpy. Refrigerate until ready to use.

3 Whisk together the milk and vinegar, allow the mixture to sit for 10 minutes, until curdled.

4 In a large bowl, whisk together the chickpea and brown rice flours, baking powder, baking soda, cinnamon, and salt; set aside.

5 In a large bowl, beat together the eggs and oil; add the sugar and beat until fully incorporated; stir in the lemon and vanilla extracts. In small batches combine the milk and flour mixtures until fully incorporated and the batter looks creamy. Fold in the blueberries (reserve a handful for the topping), and pour the batter into the prepared pan.

6 Spread the remaining blueberries evenly across the top of the batter. Remove the streusel from the refrigerator and use your fingers to break it up; sprinkle evenly across top of cake.

7 Bake for 50 to 55 minutes, until a cake tester inserted into the center comes out clean. Let the cake cool for 30 minutes and remove the sides of the pan. Let the cake cool completely before slicing.

Everyday Socca ⓥ

SERVES: 2 TO 4 AS A SIDE // **PREP TIME:** 2 TO 8 HOURS // **COOK TIME:** 12 TO 15 MINUTES

This socca recipe is a bit different than the traditional preparation that's cooked in a skillet. I cook the socca here in a large-rimmed baking sheet to make it thin and crispy throughout. While you can incorporate whatever flavors you please, like cumin or shallots, I chose to highlight a simple and delicious variation that's perfect for a small get-together or as a side to your favorite meal. Ideally, this flatbread is best served outside with a glass of chilled rosé.

1 cup (120 g) chickpea flour

1 teaspoon sea salt

Freshly ground pepper

1 cup (240 ml)
plus 1 tablespoon water

¼ cup (60 ml) extra virgin olive oil

2 garlic cloves, minced

❶ Whisk together the flour, salt, and pepper, to taste; then whisk in the water, 2 tablespoons of oil, and garlic. The batter should be the consistency of a creamy and fluid pancake batter. If the batter is too thick, add more water 1 teaspoon at a time; alternatively, if the batter is too thin, add more flour 1 teaspoon at a time. Set aside for 2 to 8 hours.

❷ Preheat oven to broil and place a baking sheet inside.

❸ When the oven is preheated, remove the baking sheet and add the remaining 2 tablespoons of oil to the pan; distribute the oil. Quickly and carefully, hold the pan in one hand and the batter in another; pour the batter while simultaneously swirling the pan to distribute the batter.

❹ Place the pan back in the lower third of the oven and bake for 12 to 15 minutes, until edges are browned and crisp. Remove from oven and slice or break up with your fingers, serve hot.

SUMMER MONTHS: JULY

115

Fried Heirloom Tomatoes ⓥ

SERVES: 2 TO 4 AS A SIDE // **PREP TIME:** 10 MINUTES // **COOK TIME:** 15 MINUTES

While fried green tomatoes are lovely and delicious, big heirloom varieties of tomatoes make for a great fried tomato as well. When battered and fried in cornmeal, their sweet flavor and juicy quality provides an irresistibly good treat. Most fried tomato variations out there call for eggs in the batter, but here chickpea batter does a great job of coating the tomato and adhering to the cornmeal. Since heirloom tomatoes can be delicate, I like frying these in small batches, about two slices per batch.

3 large heirloom tomatoes, sliced into ½-inch rounds

Coarse sea salt and freshly ground pepper

½ cup (60 g) chickpea flour

½ cup (120 ml) water

2 cups (266 g) stone-ground cornmeal

½ teaspoon red pepper flakes

½ teaspoon fine sea salt

¼ cup (60 ml) sunflower oil

Fresh thyme, to taste

❶ Lay the sliced tomatoes on a paper towel in an even layer; sprinkle both sides with coarse salt and pepper, to taste.

❷ In a shallow bowl, whisk together the flour and water until combined; set aside.

❸ In another shallow bowl, whisk together the cornmeal, red pepper flakes, fine salt, and season with pepper; set aside.

❹ Heat about 2 tablespoons of oil in a skillet over medium-high heat and prepare a plate lined with paper towels.

❺ Cook the tomatoes in batches. Once the oil is hot and shimmering, gently dip the tomatoes into the chickpea batter, and then lightly press into the cornmeal mix. Transfer to the skillet and cook for 1 to 1½ minutes, until golden, then carefully flip over and cook the other side for an additional 45 seconds to 1 minute.

❻ Transfer the tomatoes to the paper towel–lined plate to absorb excess oil. Repeat with remaining tomatoes, adding the remaining 2 tablespoons of oil as needed; serve hot and sprinkle with thyme.

Kofta Wraps with Sumac Tahini

MAKES 6 WRAPS // **PREP TIME:** 1 HOUR // **COOK TIME:** 18 TO 20 MINUTES

Kofta is traditionally a meatball consisting of beef or lamb, various warm spices, and onions, and is generally served in Middle Eastern cuisine. Each culture has a slightly different variation on it, with differences in the type of meat used, the spices added, and the sauce it's served with. The first time I had kofta was at a Palestinian restaurant in Brooklyn, where it was made with lamb and served with the tartest of tahini sauces. That dish and its harmonious flavors had a big impact on the way I thought about incorporating certain spices and flavors together. Because I'm not a big consumer of red meat these days, I wanted to have a vegetarian kofta in my back pocket for the normal day-to-day. These kofta are lentil- and rice-based, incorporate a good amount of spices that are traditionally found in a meat-based kofta, and are paired with a tart sumac tahini sauce. The toasted chickpea flour adds a mild nutty flavor, binds the kofta together, and absorbs some unwanted moisture.

KOFTA

1 cup (198 g) cooked green or brown lentils

½ cup (98 g) cooked brown rice

1 shallot, roughly chopped

1 garlic clove, roughly chopped

One ½-inch piece of ginger, peeled and minced

1 large egg, whisked

1 teaspoon coarse sea salt

½ teaspoon ground coriander

½ teaspoon ground cumin

¼ teaspoon ground allspice

¼ teaspoon ground cinnamon

½ teaspoon freshly ground pepper

⅓ cup (40 g) chickpea flour, toasted

Extra virgin olive oil, for brushing

TAHINI

¼ cup (72 g) tahini paste

¼ cup (60 ml) water

1 garlic clove, minced

1 tablespoon lemon juice

½ teaspoon sumac, plus more for garnish

¼ teaspoon fine salt

1 head butter lettuce separated for lettuce cups

¼ cup (15 g) chopped parsley and mint

1 In a food processor, pulse the lentils, rice, shallot, garlic, and ginger until broken down and chunky. Transfer to a large bowl; mix in the egg, coarse salt, spices, and pepper. Mix thoroughly, and then fold in the flour. Cover the bowl with plastic wrap and place in the refrigerator for at least 1 hour.

2 Make the tahini. Whisk together the tahini ingredients until it coats the back of a spoon and is smooth. If the sauce is too thick, add more water 1 teaspoon at a time until desired consistency is achieved. Set aside.

3 Preheat oven to 400°F (200°C) and line a baking sheet with parchment paper; set aside. Remove the kofta mixture from the refrigerator and pinch off tablespoon-size pieces. Roll in your palms to make a football-like shape, place on the parchment, and repeat with the remaining mixture. Lightly brush the tops and bottoms of the kofta with oil.

4 Bake for 17 to 20 minutes, until lightly golden. Place two kofta in each lettuce cup; drizzle generously with tahini sauce and garnish with sumac, chopped parsley, and mint. Serve warm.

Spiced Chickpea Pancakes
with Charred Corn and Radish Salsa

SERVES: 6 TO 8 // **PREP TIME:** 35 MINUTES // **COOK TIME:** 20 MINUTES

This is a savory pancake recipe that's great for serving a crowd. The idea behind them is somewhat of a riff on a Latin arepa, which is a small pancake-like dish made with corn flour. Many times arepas are served with meats or cheeses and, in some cases, with vegetables. However, I love them with vibrant summer salsas. The chickpea pancake is very much like a traditional breakfast pancake, only made without any leavening, and incorporates some savory spices. I suggest serving these pancakes warm with the cool salsa for a summer appetizer or side dish.

SALSA

2 ears of corn, husked

4 radishes, trimmed and chopped

½ jalapeño, seeds removed and minced

¼ cup chopped cilantro

Zest and juice from 1 lime

Sea salt

PANCAKES

1½ cups (360 ml) almond milk

1 tablespoon apple cider vinegar

1½ cups (180 g) chickpea flour

1 teaspoon Aleppo pepper (or chili powder)

1 teaspoon sea salt

½ teaspoon ground cumin

⅛ teaspoon freshly ground pepper

3 tablespoons extra virgin olive oil

2 large eggs

Chopped cilantro

2 tablespoons sesame seeds

① Char the corn. One at a time, hold the ear of corn over an open gas range flame or use a grill pan; use tongs to rotate the corn until blackened in spots. Repeat with remaining ear. Let the corn cool. Hold the corn vertically and use a sharp knife to cut the kernels from the cob; place the kernels in a large bowl and dispose of the cobs. Add the chopped radishes, jalapeño, cilantro, lime juice and zest, and give it all a good toss. Season with salt, and refrigerate until ready to use.

② Whisk together the milk and vinegar; let the mixture sit for 10 minutes, until surface is bubbly and curdled.

③ In a large bowl, whisk together the flour, Aleppo pepper (or chili powder), salt, cumin, and pepper. Whisk in the milk mixture, 2 tablespoons of oil, and the eggs, until no lumps remain; the mixture should resemble a thin pancake batter. Let the batter sit for at least 15 to 20 minutes, allowing for the flour to absorb the liquid and thicken a bit.

④ Heat a 10- to 12-inch skillet over medium heat; test the skillet by splashing it with water. If the water sizzles and evaporates quickly, the pan is ready. Once the skillet is hot, add 1 tablespoon olive oil.

⑤ Pour about 2 tablespoons of batter for each pancake. Be careful not to overcrowd the pan; I usually fit about 5 pancakes per batch. Cook the pancakes for about 2 minutes on each side, until you see bubbles form on the surface. Remove and place on a paper towel–lined plate to remove excess oil. Repeat with the remaining batter, adding more cooking oil as needed.

⑥ Plate the pancakes and top with the salsa, garnish with chopped cilantro and sesame seeds.

Grilled Summer Vegetables
with Chickpea Flour Dukkah ⓥ

SERVES: 4 TO 6 AS A SIDE // PREP TIME: 30 MINUTES // COOK TIME: 10 MINUTES

Dukkah is an Egyptian spice blend composed of nuts, spices, and herbs. It's traditionally served alongside crusty bread and olive oil and used for dipping; however, it's also used for breading meats and vegetables. This dukkah recipe incorporates toasted chickpea flour, which adds a fantastic nutty element that's much different than toasted nuts. The vegetables are grilled using an outdoor grill, but if you don't own one, a grill pan can be used in its place.

DUKKAH

¼ cup (30 g) chickpea flour, toasted

¼ cup (36 g) raw pistachios

2 tablespoons pine nuts

1 tablespoon coriander seeds

1½ teaspoons cumin seeds

½ teaspoon fennel seeds

½ teaspoon peppercorns

1 tablespoon plus 1½ teaspoons white sesame seeds

2 teaspoons fresh thyme

1 teaspoon sumac

½ teaspoon fine sea salt

VEGETABLES

3 tablespoons extra virgin olive oil

1 tablespoon plus 1½ teaspoons red wine vinegar

Coarse sea salt and freshly ground pepper

1 summer squash, ends trimmed and cut lengthwise

1 zucchini, ends trimmed and cut lengthwise

1 large leek, cut lengthwise, with root attached

2 medium tomatoes, each cut into 6 wedges

2 tablespoons chopped parsley

❶ To make the dukkah, heat a skillet over medium heat, add the flour and stir constantly to prevent burning. Cook for 5 to 6 minutes, until golden brown and fragrant. Place in a bowl and allow to cool.

❷ In a dry fry pan, toast the pistachios and pine nuts over medium heat until toasted and fragrant, about 2 minutes; set aside. Keep the stove on and toast the coriander, cumin, fennel, and peppercorns, until lightly golden and fragrant, about 1 to 2 minutes; place in a mortar. Last, toast the sesame seeds until lightly golden, about 1 minute, and place in the mortar. Add the toasted flour, thyme, sumac, and fine salt, and crush with a pestle until finely ground. Set aside.

❸ To prepare the vegetables, heat a grill or grill pan to moderate heat (roughly 350°F/180°C). Whisk together the oil, vinegar, and coarse salt and pepper, to taste; liberally brush over vegetables.

❹ Grill the vegetables on both sides, using tongs to turn them until light grill marks appear and the vegetables are tender (you want the vegetables tender but not mushy). Remove from the heat and let the vegetables cool until ready to handle.

❺ Transfer the vegetables to a cutting board. Cut the squash and zucchini into 1-inch size pieces. Trim the ends of the leeks and cut into ½-inch pieces. Place cut vegetables in a serving bowl and sprinkle with about 2 to 3 tablespoons of dukkah and the chopped parsley.

Cookies-and-Cream Icebox Cake ⓥ

MAKES: ONE 8-INCH ROUND CAKE // **SERVES:** 8 // **PREP TIME:** 1 HOUR // **COOK TIME:** 12 HOURS

Summertime is my least favorite time of year to bake things in a hot kitchen. But, there's one cake I love making when the temperatures rise, and that's an icebox cake. I let the thought of enduring the oven's heat fall by the wayside because this cake is totally worth it! The cookie wafers need a bit of time baking in the oven, while the whipped coconut cream takes just a few minutes to put together. Then, the cake is stacked and assembled, put in the refrigerator to set, and the next day you have a cookies 'n' cream–esque cake that's not only sweet and delicious but cold and refreshing for those hot summer days.

COOKIES

1 cup (120 g) chickpea flour

¾ cup (85 g) oat flour

¾ cup (108 g) coconut sugar

½ cup (40 g) cacao powder, plus extra for dusting

1 teaspoon psyllium husk powder

¼ teaspoon baking soda

Pinch of fine salt

¼ cup (60 ml) coconut oil, melted

1 teaspoon pure vanilla extract

¼ cup plus 1 tablespoon almond milk

CREAM

Three 13.5-ounce (398 ml each) cans coconut milk, refrigerated overnight

3 to 4 tablespoons maple syrup

1½ teaspoons pure vanilla extract

Shaved dark chocolate

❶ In a food processor, pulse the flours, sugar, cacao, baking soda, and salt until combined. Add the oil, vanilla, and ¼ cup of milk, and blend. Stop the engine and pinch the dough; if the dough is dry, add up to an additional tablespoon of milk and blend until the dough comes together. Turn the dough out onto a large piece of parchment paper, use your hands to roll into a 1½-inch log; wrap in plastic wrap and place in the refrigerator for 1 hour.

❷ Preheat oven to 350°F (180°C) and line two baking sheets with parchment paper; set aside. Slice dough into ⅛-inch coins and bake for 10 to 12 minutes, until firm; cookies will puff up when cooking, and then deflate as they cool.

❸ Remove the three cans of coconut milk from the refrigerator and place upside down. Open the cans from the bottom and pour out the coconut water. Scoop the coconut cream from the bottom of the cans and place in a large bowl. With an electric mixer on medium-high, beat the cream, 3 tablespoons of syrup, and vanilla; taste and adjust, if needed, adding more syrup for a sweeter cream.

❹ Line the bottom of an 8-inch springform pan with parchment paper. Arrange the cookies in a single layer, breaking the cookies to fill in any big gaps; layer with a generous amount of cream (about ¼ of what you have in the bowl), and spread evenly. Continue layering with wafers and cream until there are four layers of each. Cover the leftover cream with plastic wrap and reserve for later.

❺ Refrigerate overnight. When ready to serve, remove the cake and leftover cream from the refrigerator and run a thin knife around the edges of the cake, unhook the latches, and remove the sides of the pan. Use an offset spatula and spread the cream over the top and sides of the cake, covering any discoloration.

❻ Dust the cake with cacao powder and garnish with shaved chocolate and serve.

❼ Leftover cake can be stored in the refrigerator for up to 3 days.

Raspberry-Nectarine Pie
with Lemon Basil ⓥ

MAKES: ONE 8-INCH PIE // **SERVES:** 8 // **PREP TIME:** 25 MINUTES // **COOK TIME:** 50 MINUTES

Summer fruit is one of those things you want to savor forever. It seems like I am constantly wondering if that peach or blackberry I just ate will be my last of the season. While I can get kind of weepy about it, I know that next summer will be here before I know it. This pie is an easy and super delicious way to mix summer berries and stone fruit. The crust is a simple one made with a quick pulse in the food processor, pressed into a pie pan, blind baked, and then topped with fruit to go back into the oven until the fruit is hot, bubbling, and juicy. Some people might be wary of baking with chickpea flour because they think the baked good will end up tasting like a legume, but fear not! This pie is just as sweet and delicious as ever.

PIECRUST

¾ cup (79 g) gluten-free old-fashioned rolled oats

½ cup (60 g) chickpea flour

¼ cup (35g) raw pistachios

¼ teaspoon sea salt

Zest of ½ lemon

3 tablespoons plus 1 teaspoon coconut oil, melted, plus extra for brushing

2 tablespoons maple syrup

FILLING

9 ounces (260 g) ripe but firm nectarines, stones removed and cut into thin slices

1¼ cups (⅝ pint; 105 g) raspberries

2 tablespoons arrowroot powder

1 tablespoon finely chopped lemon basil

1 tablespoon plus 1½ teaspoons maple syrup

1 teaspoon lemon juice

Coconut whipped cream or ice cream (optional)

❶ In a food processor fitted with a metal S blade, pulse the oats, flour, pistachios, and salt until finely ground. Transfer to a large bowl and use a fork and mix in the lemon zest, oil, and syrup, until incorporated. Squeeze a piece of dough between your fingers; the dough should bind and stick together; if it's crumbly, add 1 teaspoon of water at a time until the dough holds together.

❷ In a separate bowl, make the filling. Combine the nectarines, 1 cup of berries, arrowroot, lemon basil, syrup, and lemon juice. Let the mixture sit to allow the arrowroot to absorb some liquid.

❸ Preheat oven to 350°F (180°C). Press the dough evenly into the tart pan using your fingertips to spread it around the bottom and up the sides. Use the tip of a fork and prick the bottom and sides of the tart; bake in the oven for 10 minutes, until slightly golden. Remove the tart and add the filling. Using a pastry brush, lightly brush the top of the fruit with melted oil. Return to the oven and bake for 30 to 35 minutes, until the fruit is bubbling. Remove from the oven and allow to cool for 20 minutes before serving. Serve with coconut whipped cream or vanilla ice cream and the remaining ¼ cup of raspberries.

Savory Zucchini, Shiso, and Black Quinoa Muffins

MAKES: 12 MUFFINS // **PREP TIME:** 35 MINUTES // **COOK TIME:** 25 MINUTES

These muffins are a great way to use zucchini, and they make for a really great breakfast or afternoon snack. The recipe is basically a take on a traditional sweet muffin, but incorporates some savory herbs, vinegar, and black quinoa. I call for shiso, also known as perilla, but if you can't find it near you, regular basil or Thai basil works just as well. Same goes for the black quinoa; I call for it because I like the contrast in color, but white or red quinoa is just as good.

½ cup (120 ml) water

¼ cup (48 g) black quinoa, rinsed

½ teaspoon plus a pinch of sea salt

½ cup (120 ml) almond milk

1 tablespoon apple cider vinegar

1 cup (120 g) chickpea flour

½ cup (50 g) almond flour

½ cup (87 g) millet flour

1 teaspoon baking powder

½ teaspoon baking soda

Freshly ground pepper

1 cup (175 g) grated zucchini

½ cup (120 ml) extra virgin olive oil

1 large egg

4 scallions, trimmed and roughly chopped

2 tablespoons minced shiso (or basil)

2 tablespoons minced parsley

1 In a small saucepan, bring the water, quinoa, and a pinch of salt to a boil over high heat; reduce the heat to low; cover the pot and cook the quinoa for 10 to 15 minutes, until water is absorbed. Set aside with cover off and allow the quinoa to cool.

2 In a liquid measure, whisk together the milk and vinegar; allow the mixture to sit for 10 minutes, until the surface is bubbly and curdled.

3 Preheat oven to 350°F (180°C) and line a twelve-cup muffin pan with liners; set aside.

4 In a large bowl, whisk together the flours, baking powder, baking soda, ½ teaspoon of salt, and pepper, to taste. Set aside.

5 In a separate bowl, combine the quinoa, milk mixture, zucchini, oil, egg, scallions, shiso, and parsley.

6 Add the dry ingredients to the wet and mix thoroughly to combine.

7 Divide the batter between the muffin liners, filling each one to the top. Bake for 25 minutes, until golden brown and a cake tester inserted into the middle of a muffin comes out clean.

8 Let the muffins cool for 15 minutes, then remove them from the muffin pan and allow them to cool completely on a rack.

Stone Fruit Breakfast Crisp
with Yogurt and Bee Pollen

SERVES: 6 TO 8 // **PREP TIME:** 25 MINUTES // **COOK TIME:** 20 TO 25 MINUTES

Fruit crisps and crumbles are the perfect summer dessert (or even breakfast) when you have an abundance of late-summer stone fruit waiting to be used up. This crisp is sweet enough for dessert, but also subtle enough for a more decadent breakfast. The chickpea flour makes having a treat like this for breakfast a high-protein option. This is also a great dish to prebake and heat up for a gathering or for leftovers.

¾ cup (90 g) chickpea flour

½ cup (52 g) gluten-free old-fashioned rolled oats

⅓ cup (30 g) slivered almonds

¼ cup (36 g) coconut sugar

Pinch of sea salt

¼ cup (60 ml) plus 2 tablespoons coconut oil, melted

2 pounds (1,000 g) firm but ripe peaches and nectarines, peeled and sliced

1 tablespoon Thai basil, finely chopped

1 tablespoon arrowroot powder

1 teaspoon lemon juice

16 ounces (454 g) coconut yogurt (or yogurt of choice)

2 tablespoons bee pollen

❶ Preheat oven to 400°F (200°C) and grease a 9-inch round pan with 2-inch sides; set aside.

❷ In a medium bowl, whisk together the flour, oats, almonds, 2 tablespoons of sugar, and salt. Drizzle in oil, and mix together with a spatula until wet and sandy. Cover with plastic wrap and set in the refrigerator for 15 minutes.

❸ In a large bowl, toss together the fruit, basil, remaining 2 tablespoons of sugar, arrowroot, and lemon juice. Set mixture aside.

❹ Remove the crumble from the refrigerator. Transfer the fruit mix to the skillet, and arrange in an even layer. Use your fingers to break up the crumble topping and distribute it evenly across the top of the fruit.

❺ Place in the center of your oven and bake for 20 to 25 minutes, until the fruit is bubbling and the topping is lightly browned. Remove from the heat and let the crumble sit for 10 minutes before serving.

❻ Serve the crumble with yogurt and divide bee pollen evenly among the servings.

Ratatouille Tartlets ⓥ

MAKES: SIX 4-INCH TARTS // **PREP TIME:** 30 MINUTES // **COOK TIME:** 1 HOUR 30 MINUTES

Ratatouille allows for using up summer's abundant vegetables. Many times I serve a similar ratatouille over quinoa or rice, but when I have the time, it makes for a great savory tart. These tarts are made with a simple dough that only requires a few pulses in your food processor. Then, the dough is pressed into the tart pans with no rolling or chilling in the refrigerator necessary. While this ratatouille is made with the usual late-summer suspects—tomatoes, eggplant, zucchini, and peppers—I love roasting the tomatoes beforehand and then adding them to the rest of the sautéed vegetables to add a sweet, roasted flavor that really comes through.

TARTS

1½ cups (157 g) gluten-free old-fashioned rolled oats

1 cup (120 g) chickpea flour

½ cup (70 g) sunflower seeds

2 tablespoons sesame seeds

1 teaspoon fine sea salt

¼ teaspoon freshly ground pepper

½ cup (120 ml) extra virgin olive oil

¼ cup (60 ml) ice water

RATATOUILLE

One 28-ounce (794 g) can peeled whole tomatoes, drained

1 cup (149 g) grape or cherry tomatoes

¼ cup (60 ml) extra virgin olive oil

Coarse sea salt and freshly ground pepper

1 medium onion, diced

2 Japanese eggplants, sliced in half and cut into ⅓-inch slices

2 zucchinis, sliced in half and cut into ⅓-inch slices

1 red bell pepper, diced

¼ cup (5 g) basil, julienned

2 tablespoons chopped oregano

1 teaspoon red wine vinegar

① Preheat oven to 350°F (180°C). Lightly grease six tartlet pans and place them on a baking sheet; set aside. In a food processor fitted with a metal S blade, pulse together the oats, flour, seeds, fine salt, and pepper until finely ground, about 30 seconds. Place the pulsed mixture in a large bowl; pour in the oil and water; mix thoroughly with a fork until mixture is wet and clumpy. Divide the dough evenly among the tart pans, pressing the dough into the bottoms and sides. Bake for 30 minutes, until golden brown. Remove from the oven and let cool completely. (Keep oven at 350°F/180°C for the tomatoes).

② To make the ratatouille, line a baking sheet with parchment paper and place the peeled tomatoes on the sheet; use your hands to squash them, letting their juices release; toss in cherry tomatoes, 1 tablespoon of oil, and season with coarse salt and pepper. Bake for 30 to 35 minutes, stirring halfway through, until the crushed tomatoes have thickened and the cherry tomatoes are wrinkled and soft. Remove from the oven and set aside.

③ While the tomatoes are cooking, heat 2 tablespoons of oil in a large skillet over medium heat. Add the onion and stir; cook until soft and translucent, about 5 minutes. Add the eggplants and 1 tablespoon of oil, and stir until softened, roughly 5 minutes. Transfer the onion and eggplant to a large bowl and return the pan to the heat.

④ Add the zucchini and bell pepper to the pan, season with coarse salt and pepper, and stir until softened, about 10 minutes. Stir in the tomatoes, basil, and oregano, and cook for 10 more minutes, until all the vegetables are tender, but still hold their form. Stir the eggplant and onion back into mixture, and stir in the vinegar; season with coarse salt and pepper. Set aside for a few minutes to cool.

⑤ Divide the warm ratatouille among the tart shells and serve.

Sweet Corn and Cilantro Chowder ⓥ

SERVES: 6 TO 8 // **PREP TIME:** 30 MINUTES // **COOK TIME:** 35 TO 40 MINUTES

This chowder is perfect for a busy night, since the ingredients can readily be found at the market this time of year or in your pantry. Like most chowders, this one is thick and creamy and full of sweet corn, chunks of potato, and bits of charred poblano pepper. The chickpea flour acts more as a flavor element than a thickener, although it does help in that department as well. It lends this traditional chowder a bit of nuttiness that it would otherwise not have. You can use light coconut milk here if you prefer a lower fat content. Serve this alongside some crackers or torn bread on a cool, perhaps overcast summer day.

¼ cup (30 g) chickpea flour

2 tablespoons coconut oil

1 large onion, diced

1 poblano pepper, seeds and ribs removed, diced

2 garlic cloves, minced

1½ teaspoons crushed cumin seeds (or ground cumin)

4 cups (960 ml) vegetable broth

1 cup (240 ml) coconut milk, plus more for garnish

2 small potatoes, cut into ½-inch chunks

Kernels from 4 ears of corn, 2 cobs reserved

Sea salt and freshly ground pepper

¼ cup (5 g) cilantro, finely chopped, plus more for garnish

1 tablespoon fresh lime juice, plus lime wedges for garnish

Pinch of cayenne

❶ Heat a skillet over medium heat. Once the pan is hot, add the flour. Toast for 7 to 8 minutes, stirring often to prevent burning, until the flour is golden and fragrant. Place the flour in a bowl to cool. Set aside.

❷ Heat the oil in a large soup pot over medium heat; once hot, add the onion and pepper; stir and cook until the pepper is soft and the onion is translucent in color, about 5 to 7 minutes.

❸ Add the garlic, cumin, and toasted flour, stir, and cook for 30 seconds, until the garlic is fragrant. Add the broth, milk, potatoes, two cobs, and salt and pepper, to taste; turn the heat to high and bring to a boil. Cover the pot and turn the heat down to a simmer; cook until the potatoes are tender when poked with a sharp knife, about 20 minutes.

❹ Add the corn kernels and cook until tender, about 5 minutes. Turn the heat off and let the soup cool for a few minutes before blending.

❺ Ladle half the soup into a blender, puree, and add back to the soup pot. Stir in the cilantro. Taste and adjust seasoning, then add the lime juice.

❻ Divide the chowder among bowls, and drizzle with extra milk; top with chopped cilantro and a pinch of cayenne. Serve with a side of lime wedges.

Eggplant Schnitzel Plate

SERVES: 4 TO 6 // **PREP TIME:** 20 MINUTES // **COOK TIME:** 20 MINUTES

This is a quick, pantry-based recipe that requires minimal time and utilizes late-summer eggplant and tomatoes in a satisfying meal. The eggplant is breaded in chickpea flour and bread crumbs and baked until tender and crisp. It's served warm with a simple parsley and tomato toss, lightly dressed in lemon and olive oil. These are the kinds of summer dishes I love to cook—fresh, requiring minimal effort, and flavorful.

2 to 3 teaspoons extra virgin olive oil, plus more for brushing

2 large eggplants, cut lengthwise into ½-inch slices

½ teaspoon sea salt, plus more to taste

Freshly ground pepper

1 large egg

¼ cup (60 ml) almond milk

½ cup (60 g) chickpea flour, toasted

1 cup (132 g) gluten-free fine bread crumbs of choice

1 pound (470 g) heirloom cherry tomatoes, halved

1½ cups (20 g) parsley, tough stems removed and roughly chopped

1 to 2 teaspoons lemon juice, plus lemon wedges for garnish

Handful of microgreens

1 Preheat oven to 400°F (200°C), and line two baking sheets with parchment paper; brush the parchment with oil to coat and set aside.

2 Lay the eggplant slices on a large dish towel and sprinkle liberally with salt and pepper. Let them sit for 20 minutes, turning them over halfway through to release some of their moisture.

3 In a shallow bowl, combine the egg and milk; whisk and set aside.

4 In another shallow bowl, combine the flour, bread crumbs, and ½ teaspoon of salt. Set aside.

5 Dip the eggplant into the egg mixture, letting excess drip off, and then press into the flour mixture to coat evenly. Place on the baking sheet. Repeat with remaining eggplant slices.

6 Bake the eggplant for 10 minutes, remove from the oven, flip over, and bake for another 10 minutes, until the eggplant slices are tender and the breading is golden brown.

7 While the eggplant is cooking, toss together the tomatoes and parsley, drizzle in lemon juice and the 2 to 3 teaspoons of oil, and season with salt and pepper; set aside.

8 Serve the eggplant hot, with a side of the parsley and tomato toss, lemon wedges, and microgreens.

Grilled Vegetable Kebabs
with Green Goddess Sauce ⓥ

SERVES: 4 // **PREP TIME:** 45 MINUTES // **COOK TIME:** 10 MINUTES

Grilling vegetables is something I wish I could do year-round. It's a great way to add unique flavor, and there's easy cleanup! I love pairing grilled vegetables with zingy sauces or punchy dressings, and because chickpea flour is wonderful in sauces as a thickening agent, I found it to be perfect as the base for a dairy-free green goddess sauce.

SAUCE

¼ cup (15 g) packed parsley

2 tablespoons chopped basil

2 tablespoons chopped dill

2 tablespoons extra virgin olive oil

1 tablespoon lemon juice

1 tablespoon chopped mint

1 tablespoon chopped oregano

1 garlic clove

2 teaspoons apple cider vinegar

1 cup (240 ml) water

¼ cup (30 g) chickpea flour

2 tablespoons tahini paste

½ teaspoon sea salt

Freshly ground pepper

KEBABS

14 ounces (411 g) new potatoes (or fingerling)

3 medium summer squash

½ red onion

Extra virgin olive oil, for brushing

Sea salt and freshly ground pepper

¼ cup (15 g) chopped chives (optional)

① In a food processor fitted with a metal S blade, puree the parsley, basil, dill, oil, lemon juice, mint, oregano, garlic, and vinegar; set aside.

② In a saucepan, whisk together the water and flour until no lumps remain. Turn the heat to medium and continue whisking until the mixture thickens and has a pudding-like consistency, 6 to 7 minutes. Remove the pan from the heat and carefully pour the flour mixture into the food processor; blend until thoroughly incorporated. Add the tahini paste, salt, and pepper, to taste. Taste and adjust salt and/or lemon juice, if needed. Pour the sauce into a bowl and let it rest while you prepare the skewers.

③ Soak the wood skewers in water for at least 30 minutes, and set aside.

④ Place the potatoes in a saucepan and fill with water to cover about 1 inch above potatoes; bring to a boil, then turn down to a simmer and cook for 10 minutes, until the potatoes can easily be pierced with a sharp knife. Drain the potatoes and let cool.

⑤ Cut the ends off the squash and into 1-inch chunks; set aside. Peel the onion and cut into ½-inch pieces.

⑥ Heat the grill to medium-high (roughly 300°F/150°C to 350°F/180°C). Thread the potatoes, squash, and onion onto the skewers, alternating between each vegetable. Brush liberally with oil, and season with salt and pepper.

⑦ Grill the kebabs, turning every few minutes, until the vegetables have light grill marks and are tender, roughly 5 to 7 minutes. Remove from the heat and place on a serving platter.

⑧ Mix the sauce; at this point it should have thickened and cooled. If the sauce thickened too much, blend water in, a teaspoon at a time, until you reach your desired consistency.

⑨ Drizzle the sauce over the vegetables and serve warm with chopped chives.

Blackberry-Lime Cobbler

SERVES: 8 // **PREP TIME:** 10 MINUTES // **COOK TIME:** 30 TO 35 MINUTES

Using really fresh fruit makes all the difference in a cobbler. So I would suggest saving this recipe for a time when blackberries are at their height where you live. The topping here is more of a light cake that bakes on top of the berries, lightly encasing them in batter. This makes for a great dessert when entertaining a crowd or for a family cookout. It's even more wonderful served with a big scoop of vanilla ice cream.

2¼ pints (1,020 g) blackberries

¼ cup (36 g) plus 2 tablespoons coconut sugar

¼ cup (30 g) plus 1 tablespoon arrowroot powder

Zest from ½ lime, plus 1 tablespoon lime juice

¾ cup (90 g) chickpea flour

¼ cup (27 g) sorghum flour

1 teaspoon baking powder

½ teaspoon baking soda

½ teaspoon sea salt

⅓ cup (80 ml) almond milk

3 tablespoons sunflower oil

1 large egg

½ teaspoon pure vanilla extract

❶ Preheat oven to 375°F (190°C) and grease a 9 x 13-inch pan; set aside.

❷ In a bowl, gently toss together the blackberries, 2 tablespoons sugar, 1 tablespoon arrowroot, and lime juice and zest; set aside to let flavors combine and arrowroot to absorb some liquid.

❸ In a separate bowl, whisk together the flours, the remaining ¼ cup of arrowroot, the remaining ¼ cup of sugar, baking powder, baking soda, and salt. In a small bowl, whisk together the milk, oil, egg, and vanilla.

❹ Evenly spread the berries across the bottom of the prepared pan. Use a spoon to scoop bunches of the batter over the top of the berries. Bake for 30 to 35 minutes, until the fruit is bubbling and the topping is golden brown. Allow the cobbler to cool for 10 minutes before serving.

Sweet Flatbread with Grilled Berries ⓥ

MAKES: 4 FLATBREADS // **PREP TIME:** 20 MINUTES // **COOK TIME:** 20 MINUTES

While summer berries are vibrant and delicious at this time of year, I really love roasting or grilling them until they're just bursting and overflowing with their sweet juices. Grilling berries, especially over a charcoal grill, contributes a slight smokiness that you can't get when roasting them in the oven. When I first grilled berries it was a spur-of-the-moment decision that has influenced my summer cookouts from that point on. These flatbreads lend themselves to preparing after the sun has set and the temperatures feel a bit more inviting to eat something warm.

FLATBREAD

1 cup (120 g) chickpea flour

1 tablespoon plus 1½ teaspoons cane sugar

½ teaspoon ground cinnamon

Pinch of sea salt

1 tablespoon coconut oil, melted

1 tablespoon unsweetened coconut yogurt

2 tablespoons almond milk

Sorghum flour, for dusting

BERRIES

3 cups (410 g) mixed berries

2 tablespoons maple syrup

1 tablespoon lemon juice

1 teaspoon arrowroot powder

¼ teaspoon coconut oil, melted

Zest from ½ lemon

Dairy-free vanilla ice cream

❶ In a large bowl, whisk together the chickpea flour, sugar, cinnamon, and salt. Drizzle in the oil and yogurt; use your fingers to distribute throughout the flour until crumbly. A tablespoon at a time, drizzle the milk into the flour mixture, using your fingers to mix it into the dough; the dough should come together into a uniform ball. Knead the dough until smooth and springy, about 3 minutes. Place the dough on a clean surface and cover with a damp dish towel; let rest for 10 minutes.

❷ While the dough is resting, prepare the berries and heat the grill.* In a large bowl, toss the berries, syrup, lemon juice, arrowroot, oil, and zest. Transfer the berry mixture to a heavy-duty sheet of aluminum foil and fold up the sides to make a foil packet. Set aside.

❸ Divide the dough into four even pieces and roll the dough into balls, place to the side, and cover with a dish towel. Place a large piece of parchment on an even work surface, and dust it with sorghum flour. Place one ball of dough on the parchment, dust with more flour, and flatten with your palm to make a disk. One at a time, roll each piece of dough into a 6-inch round, turning and dusting with flour to prevent sticking. Set aside.

❹ Heat a skillet over medium-high heat. When hot, place the dough onto the dry skillet and cook for 45 seconds to 1 minute, until you see white bubbles form on top of the dough. Gently flip the dough over and cook for another 40 to 45 seconds. Remove from the pan and set aside; repeat with remaining dough.

❺ Grill should be producing moderate heat, approximately 400°F (200°C). Place the berry packet over the heat and allow the berries to cook for 7 to 10 minutes, until bubbling and hot; remove from the grill.

❻ Plate the flatbreads and top with ice cream and the hot berries.

*Note: If you don't own or have access to a grill, roast the aluminum foil berry packet in your oven at 400°F (200°C) for 10 to 12 minutes until juicy and bubbling.

Goji Berry and Cacao Nib Granola Bars Ⓥ

MAKES: 8 BARS // **PREP TIME:** 10 MINUTES // **COOK TIME:** 18 TO 20 MINUTES

My ideal breakfast bar is one that's filling enough to last me throughout the morning but one that's not overly sweet. These bars strike a balance between the two, as they are nourishing without losing any flavor. They have tons of texture, a hint of sweetness; they're more on the chewy side, but definitely hide crunchy cacao nibs and chopped nuts in each bite. They're perfect for a quick breakfast on the go or to take on a long road trip or plane ride, since they pack easily and aren't sensitive to heat.

1 cup (120 g) chickpea flour

1 cup (20 g) puffed brown rice

1 cup (105 g) gluten-free old-fashioned rolled oats

½ cup (70 g) almonds, roughly chopped

¼ cup (37 g) cacao nibs

¼ cup (30 g) chopped dried goji berries

¼ cup (30 g) sunflower seeds

1 teaspoon ground cinnamon

1 teaspoon sea salt

½ cup (120 g) smooth almond butter

½ cup (100 g) applesauce

⅓ cup (80 ml) plus 1 tablespoon brown rice syrup

2 tablespoons coconut oil, melted

½ teaspoon pure vanilla extract

❶ Preheat oven to 350°F (180°C) and line an 8 x 8-inch square pan with parchment paper, making sure it's long enough to hang over sides. Set aside.

❷ In a large bowl, whisk together the flour, rice, oats, almonds, nibs, berries, seeds, cinnamon, and salt. In another bowl, whisk together the almond butter, applesauce, syrup, oil, and vanilla.

❸ Pour the wet ingredients into the dry mix and combine thoroughly with a rubber spatula. Transfer the mix to the prepared pan, and use the back of the spatula to spread the mixture evenly into corners and sides of the pan. Bake for 18 to 20, until the top is golden brown.

❹ Let cool completely before slicing.

Fig and Hazelnut Clafoutis

MAKES: ONE 9-INCH CLAFOUTIS // **SERVES:** 4 TO 6 // **PREP TIME:** 20 MINUTES
COOK TIME: 45 TO 50 MINUTES

The clafoutis may have an intimidating name, but it couldn't be easier to put together or be more impressive to serve. It's similar in look to a Dutch baby pancake but is sweeter and doesn't rise as much. It's French in origin and traditionally baked with cherries and served as a sweet breakfast or as a brunch option with a smattering of confectioners' sugar. Figs are a favorite of mine this time of year; they are not only ripe and at their peak but taste wonderful when baked and served warm with this slightly sweet dish.

1 cup (240 ml) coconut milk

1 tablespoon apple cider vinegar

3 large eggs

¼ cup (55 g) cane sugar

1 teaspoon pure vanilla extract

½ teaspoon lemon zest

¼ cup (30 g) plus 2 tablespoons chickpea flour

2 tablespoons hazelnut flour

¼ teaspoon sea salt

¾ pound figs, halved lengthwise

Confectioners' sugar, for dusting

❶ Preheat oven to 375°F (190°C) and grease a 9-inch pan; set aside.

❷ Whisk together the milk and vinegar; let the mixture sit for 10 minutes. In a bowl, whisk together the milk mixture, eggs, sugar, vanilla, and zest. Add the flours and salt; whisk until smooth. Pour the batter into the prepared pan and top with the figs, cut side up. Bake for 45 to 50 minutes, until a cake tester inserted into the center comes out clean.

❸ Remove from the heat and let cool slightly, dust with confectioners' sugar, and serve.

Baked Squash Tempura with Hemp Dip

SERVES: 4 TO 6 // **PREP TIME:** 12 HOURS // **COOK TIME:** 20 MINUTES

Tempura batter is a favorite of mine; it has a supremely light texture, a subtle flavor, and is really simple to prepare. While tempura is traditionally fried, I have found that baking it delivers a very similar outcome: light and crispy, with a tender center. The chickpea flour batter provides a hearty but unique taste here. Because tempura has such a delicate flavor, I paired it with a bold dip with a creamy base composed of cashews, hemp seeds, and miso paste. There are quite a few other pantry ingredients needed and some soaking time involved, so preparing the dip requires a little bit of planning ahead.

DIP

¼ cup (44 g) cashews, soaked overnight and drained

¼ cup (32 g) hemp seed hearts

¼ cup (60 ml) water

2 tablespoons extra virgin olive oil

1 tablespoon gluten-free mellow white miso

2½ teaspoons rice wine vinegar

2 teaspoons Dijon mustard

1 teaspoon tamari

1 garlic clove, roughly chopped

¼ teaspoon maple syrup

¼ teaspoon sea salt

Freshly ground pepper

TEMPURA

Olive oil cooking spray

¾ cup (90 g) chickpea flour

½ cup (60 g) arrowroot powder

½ teaspoon sea salt

1 cup (240 ml) ice water

1 large egg

1 acorn squash (1,000 g), cut into quarters and sliced ¼-inch thick

2 tablespoons chopped parsley

❶ Add the dip ingredients to a high-speed blender; blend on high until the dip is smooth and creamy. Transfer to a lidded jar and refrigerate for 1 hour or until ready to use.

❷ Preheat oven to 450°F (230°C) and line two baking sheets with parchment paper. Spray the paper with a good coating of olive oil cooking spray (if you do not have spray oil, brush each paper-lined baking sheet with 1 tablespoon of olive oil); set aside.

❸ In a large bowl, whisk together the flour, arrowroot, and salt. Whisk in the water and egg until incorporated; batter should be the consistency of a crepe batter.

❹ Dip the squash pieces into the batter, letting excess batter drip off; place on the prepared baking sheets. Bake for 10 to 12 minutes, until the edges of the squash are sizzling and the bottoms are lightly golden. Remove from the oven and gently flip each piece over; place back in the oven for 7 minutes, until the squash is lightly browned and tender.

❺ Serve immediately with hemp dip and sprinkle with parsley.

Creamy Harvest Tabbouleh Salad ⓥ

SERVES: 6 TO 8 AS A SIDE // **PREP TIME:** 20 MINUTES // **COOK TIME:** 40 MINUTES

I use the term "tabbouleh" very loosely here, but that's what this recipe was inspired by. Traditional tabbouleh is often prepared with tomatoes, onion, and herbs, and is made with bulgur and in some cases couscous, both of which contain gluten. My go-to gluten-free replacements are millet and quinoa, and since this is a late-summer salad, it's full of fresh butternut squash, kale ribbons, tart and crunchy apples, and a warm and creamy chickpea flour–based dressing.

DRESSING

¼ cup (60 ml) extra virgin olive oil

1 medium shallot, roughly chopped

1 tablespoon sherry vinegar

2 teaspoons Dijon mustard

¼ teaspoon sea salt

⅛ teaspoon freshly ground pepper

¼ cup (60 ml) water

2 tablespoons chickpea flour

SALAD

1 small butternut squash, peeled and cut into ½-inch cubes

1½ teaspoons extra virgin olive oil

Coarse sea salt and freshly ground pepper

2 cups (480 ml) water

1 cup (185 g) millet

Fine salt

2 large leaves Lacinato or dinosaur kale, finely shredded

½ apple, cored and sliced thin (Honeycrisp preferred)

¼ cup (33 g) toasted cashews, roughly chopped

❶ Make the sauce. Place the oil, shallot, vinegar, mustard, salt, and pepper in an upright blender (or use an immersion blender); blend for 30 seconds, until the shallot has broken down. In a small saucepan, whisk together the water and flour until no lumps remain. Turn the heat to medium-low and whisk every few seconds until the mixture has thickened to the consistency of a roux or melted cheese, about 2 minutes. Quickly transfer the mixture to the blender (or bowl with an immersion blender); blend on high for 1 minute, stopping to scrape down the sides, until the sauce is creamy. Set aside to cool while you prepare the tabbouleh.

❷ Preheat oven to 400°F (200°C) and line a rimmed baking sheet with parchment paper; set aside. In a bowl, toss the squash, oil, and coarse salt and pepper, to taste, until the squash cubes are evenly coated; turn out onto the prepared baking sheet and cook for 15 to 20 minutes, until the squash is tender and the edges are lightly golden. Set aside.

❸ While the squash is cooking, combine the water, millet, and a big pinch of fine salt in a saucepan. Bring to a boil and stir; turn the heat down to low, cover the pot, and simmer for 15 to 20 minutes, until no more water remains and millet is tender. Let the millet sit for 10 minutes, then fluff with a fork.

❹ In a large serving bowl, combine the millet, squash, kale, apple, and cashews. Fold in all the dressing and combine thoroughly. Adjust the salt and pepper, if needed, and serve warm.

Loaded Sweet Potatoes
with Chickpea Sour Cream ⓥ

MAKES: 1½ CUPS SOUR CREAM // **SERVES:** 4 TO 8 // **PREP TIME:** 12 HOURS // **COOK TIME:** 2 HOURS

These loaded sweet potatoes are a perfect meal on their own or a great dish to serve as a side. The sour cream is chickpea flour–based and needs a good day or so to cool and set up, so planning to make it ahead of time is something to consider. It can be made 2 days before serving, and lasts about 5 days in the refrigerator. Once the cream does set, you can use it to top just about anything as you would with traditional sour cream.

SOUR CREAM

¼ cup (33 g) plus 1 tablespoon cashews, soaked overnight and drained

2 teaspoons apple cider vinegar

1 teaspoon lemon juice

½ teaspoon Dijon mustard

½ teaspoon sea salt

1 cup (240 ml) water

¼ cup (30 g) chickpea flour

POTATOES

4 medium sweet potatoes

One 15-ounce (425 g) can chickpeas, drained and rinsed

½ cup (120 ml) plus 1½ teaspoons extra virgin olive oil

1 teaspoon sumac

1 teaspoon sea salt, plus more to taste

Freshly ground pepper

1 bunch scallions, ends trimmed and white and light green parts sliced thin

Handful of microgreens

❶ Make the sour cream ahead of time so that way it's ready when you want to use it. Place the cashews, vinegar, lemon juice, mustard, and salt in an upright high-speed blender. In a small saucepan, whisk together the water and flour until no lumps remain. Turn the heat to medium and continue to whisk every few seconds. At around 4 minutes, the mixture will begin steaming and will get increasingly creamy; keep whisking for another 2 to 3 minutes, until thickened (like the consistency of a roux or a thin pudding). Quickly and carefully, pour the hot mixture into the blender; blend on high for 1 minute, scraping down the sides as you go along. Taste and adjust any seasonings. Place in a lidded jar and let cool with the top off, stirring every 10 minutes or so until cool. Cover with a lid and place in the refrigerator until ready to use.

❷ Preheat oven to 400°F (200°C) and line a baking sheet with parchment paper. Pierce the potatoes with a fork and place on the baking sheet; bake for 1 hour, until potatoes can be easily pierced with a sharp knife. Remove from the oven and let cool.

❸ While the potatoes are baking, toss the chickpeas with 1½ teaspoons of oil, sumac, salt, and pepper, to taste. In the last 25 minutes of the potatoes baking, add the chickpeas and cook for 25 to 30 minutes, until the chickpeas are crisp and lightly browned.

❹ Slice the potatoes in half; use a fork to mash about 1 tablespoon of oil and a few pinches of salt into the flesh of each. Remove the sour cream from the refrigerator and give it a stir; top the potatoes with sour cream, chickpeas, sliced scallions, and a handful of microgreens.

Quinoa Falafel with Romesco Sauce ⓥ

MAKES: 1 CUP ROMESCO SAUCE AND 32 FALAFELS // **SERVES:** 4 // **PREP TIME:** 1 HOUR 30 MINUTES
COOK TIME: 20 TO 25 MINUTES

Falafel may be one of the most versatile and customizable foods out there. There are so many variations, whether you're looking on the Web or in various cookbooks. Some recipes use cooked millet, are pulsed with kale for green falafel, or made with beans other than chickpeas; and some falafel are baked rather than fried. This basic falafel is my favorite. It has the perfect balance of flavors and spices, hold together without being mushy or moist, and incorporate toasted chickpea flour to bind them, but also for a nutty flavor.

ROMESCO SAUCE

2 red bell peppers

1 garlic clove, roughly chopped

¼ cup (60 ml) extra virgin olive oil

2 tablespoons hazelnuts, toasted and skins removed

1 tablespoon tahini paste

2 teaspoons apple cider vinegar

¾ teaspoon smoked paprika

¼ teaspoon sea salt

⅛ teaspoon cayenne (optional)

FALAFEL

½ cup (95 g) quinoa, rinsed

1 cup (240 ml) plus 3 tablespoons water

½ cup (100 g) whole mung beans

1 tablespoon ground flaxseed meal

½ cup (15 g) parsley, plus extra for serving

¼ cup (30 g) chickpea flour, toasted

1 shallot, roughly chopped

2 garlic cloves, roughly chopped

1 tablespoon lemon juice

2 teaspoons sea salt

1½ teaspoons ground cumin

1½ teaspoons ground nutmeg

1 teaspoon paprika

½ teaspoon ground turmeric

1 tablespoon black sesame seeds

Extra virgin olive oil, for brushing

1 Turn oven to broil and line a rimmed baking sheet with parchment paper.

2 Place the peppers on the baking sheet and broil, turning over every 30 seconds, until skins are blackened in spots. Place the peppers in a large bowl; cover tightly with plastic wrap for 10 minutes. Peel the peppers' skins with your fingers.

3 Cut the peppers, removing the white ribs and seeds; then rinse the peppers and pat dry. Place the peppers, garlic, oil, hazelnuts, tahini, vinegar, paprika, salt, and cayenne (if using) in a food processor. Blend until smooth and creamy. Transfer the sauce to a bowl and cover with plastic wrap until ready to use. (Rinse food processor and set aside.)

4 Cook the quinoa with 1 cup of water for 12 to 14 minutes, until cooked and water has evaporated; set aside. Fill a small saucepan three-quarters of the way with water, add the mung beans and bring to a boil; turn heat down to a simmer and cook for 25 to 30 minutes, until tender and doubled in size; drain any remaining water and set aside.

5 In a small bowl, whisk together the flaxseed and 3 tablespoons of water; let mixture sit for 10 minutes, until thick.

6 In the food processor, add the cooked quinoa, mung beans, flaxseed mixture, parsley, flour, shallots, garlic, lemon juice, salt, and spices. Blend until thoroughly combined; taste for salt and lemon and adjust if necessary. Transfer to a large bowl and stir in the sesame seeds; cover with plastic wrap and refrigerate for 1 hour or overnight.

7 Preheat oven to 375°F (190°C) and line two baking sheets with parchment paper; set aside.

8 Pinch off a golf ball–size piece of mixture and roll between palms to shape into a ball. Place on prepared baking sheet and repeat.

9 Lightly brush the tops and bottoms of the falafel with oil. Bake for 20 to 25 minutes, rotating the baking sheets and flipping falafels over halfway through the baking time.

10 Serve warm with romesco sauce and garnish with parsley.

Chewy Olive Oil Chocolate Chip Cookies with Pink Himalayan Salt

MAKES: 18 COOKIES // **PREP TIME:** 1 HOUR 10 MINUTES // **COOK TIME:** 16 TO 18 MINUTES

Chocolate chip cookies are a personal, if not a very subjective, treat. Some people like them with chocolate chunks as opposed to chocolate chips; some recipes call for three types of sugar, some for various flours; then there are vegan chocolate chip cookies, grain-free, or gluten-free cookies. While I won't presume these will be everyone's ideal chocolate chip cookie, they are one of the best I've ever eaten. They bake up thin, are crisp on the edges, and are chewy on the inside. There are chunks of melted chocolate riddled throughout, and, while they are certainly sweet, the olive oil gives them an earthy tone.

¾ cup (90 g) chickpea flour

¾ cup (85 g) oat flour

1 teaspoon baking powder

¾ teaspoon sea salt

½ teaspoon baking soda

1 cup (144 g) coconut sugar

½ cup (120 ml) extra virgin olive oil

1 large egg

1 tablespoon almond milk

1 teaspoon pure vanilla extract

6 ounces (170 g) roughly chopped bittersweet chocolate (60 to 70 percent cacao)

A few pinches pink Himalayan salt

❶ In a large bowl, whisk together the flours, baking powder, salt, and baking soda. In a separate bowl, use an electric mixer to beat the sugar and oil together; beat in the egg, milk, and vanilla until combined; mixture will be thick and sticky. Add chocolate and fold in with a rubber spatula. Cover the bowl with plastic wrap and refrigerate for 1 hour.

❷ Forty minutes into the cookie dough chilling in the refrigerator, preheat the oven to 350°F (180°C) and line two cookie sheets with parchment paper; set aside.

❸ Using a tablespoon measure, scoop out the cookie dough and place on the prepared baking sheet, leaving 2 inches between cookies.

❹ Bake the cookies for 16 to 18 minutes, rotating them top to bottom and front to back, until lightly browned. Remove from the oven and sprinkle with salt.

❺ Let the cookies cool for 15 minutes before serving. Cookies can be stored at room temperature in a lidded container for 3 to 4 days.

A Late-Summer Birthday Cake

MAKES: ONE 2-LAYER CAKE // **SERVES:** 8 // **PREP TIME:** 12 HOURS // **COOK TIME:** 35 TO 40 MINUTES

Birthday cake has always been a big deal to me. Growing up, my mom made sure to bake me a homemade chocolate birthday cake with chocolate frosting. I've tried to carry that tradition on each year with my husband, since our birthdays are within days of each other's. Luckily we're both chocolate lovers, but this version of my beloved chocolate cake is perhaps my most favorite, with a blackberry jam between the layers. It's a tried-and-true cake recipe that's moist and tender and perfect to eat alone or under a good amount of frosting.

BLACKBERRY CHIA SEED JAM

1 pint (170 g) blackberries, with extra reserved for topping

1 to 2 tablespoons maple syrup

2 tablespoons chia seeds

1 teaspoon pure vanilla extract

CHOCOLATE MOUSSE

¾ cup (106 g) raw macadamia nuts, soaked overnight and drained

¼ cup (60 ml) almond milk

¼ cup (33 g) raw cashews, soaked overnight and drained

¼ cup (60 ml) coconut oil, melted

¼ cup (60 ml) maple syrup

2 tablespoons raw cacao powder

2 ounces (57 g) bittersweet chocolate (60 to 70 percent cacao), melted

1 teaspoon pure vanilla extract

Pinch of salt

CAKE

1 cup (140 g) brown rice flour

1 cup (120 g) chickpea flour

1½ cups (216 g) coconut sugar

½ cup (40 g) raw cacao powder

2 teaspoons baking powder

1 teaspoon baking soda

1 teaspoon psyllium husk powder

½ teaspoon sea salt

½ cup (120 ml) coconut oil, melted and cooled

2 large eggs

1 Make the blackberry chia seed jam ahead. Add the blackberries and syrup to a small saucepan over medium heat; stir constantly to prevent scorching. Use the back of a wooden spoon to break the berries down, and cook until the berries are soft and bubbling; about 10 minutes. Turn the heat off and stir in the chia seeds and vanilla until combined; pour into a lidded jar and allow to come to room temperature before storing in the refrigerator. Chia seed jam can be stored in the refrigerator for up to 1 week.

2 In a high-speed blender, combine the macadamias, milk, cashews, oil, syrup, cacao, chocolate, vanilla, and salt; blend on high, stopping to scrape down the sides as needed, until the mousse is smooth (if needed, add up to 1 tablespoon extra almond milk if you can't get the mousse to blend; this should help you achieve a silkier mousse). Transfer to a lidded container and store in the refrigerator until about 30 minutes prior to using.

3 Preheat oven to 350°F (180°C). Grease two 8-inch round cake pans (make sure they are at least 2 inches tall), and line the bottoms with parchment paper; set aside.

4 In a large bowl, whisk together the flours, sugar, cacao, baking powder, baking soda, psyllium husk, and salt. In another large bowl, whisk together the oil, eggs, milks, and vanilla. Mix the wet ingredients into the dry until thoroughly combined.

5 Evenly divide the batter between the cake pans and bake for 35 to 40 minutes, until a cake tester inserted into the center of each layer comes out clean. Remove from the oven and place the cakes on a rack and let them cool completely.

6 Once the cakes are cool, invert each of them onto a piece of plastic wrap and refrigerate for at least 2 hours or overnight.

7 When ready to make the frosting, remove the coconut milk from the refrigerator and turn the can upside down; open the can from the bottom and pour the coconut water from the can. Scoop out the

Recipe continues . . .

1 cup (240 ml) almond milk

1 cup (240 ml) coconut milk

2 teaspoons pure vanilla extract

FROSTING

One 13.5-ounce (398 ml) can coconut milk, refrigerated overnight

2 tablespoons raw cacao powder

1 to 2 tablespoons maple syrup

2 teaspoons pure vanilla extract

solidified coconut cream from the can and place in a bowl; beat in the cacao, syrup, and vanilla with an electric mixer on high until stiff and fluffy. Taste and adjust sweetness, adding more syrup by the ½ teaspoon if necessary. Cover with plastic wrap and place in the refrigerator until ready to use.

8 When ready to assemble the cake, remove the mousse from the refrigerator and let it come to room temperature, about 30 minutes. Remove the cake layers, blackberry chia seed jam, and chocolate-coconut frosting from the refrigerator.*

9 Place one cake layer on a cake stand or platter (use whatever you will be using to serve the cake on), and spread about a ½-inch layer of mousse (reserve leftover mousse for later). Scoop out the blackberry chia seed jam and spread an even layer over the top of the mousse, leaving a ½-inch border on the sides. Place the remaining cake layer on top; using an offset spatula, use the remaining mousse to fill in any gaps between the bottom and top layer.

10 Use your offset spatula to spread the chocolate-coconut frosting over the top and sides of cake. Decorate the top with extra blackberries and serve.

11 Cake can be refrigerated for up to 2 hours uncovered. If you are planning to refrigerate longer, drape a large piece of parchment paper over the top. Leftover cake can be refrigerated for up to 3 to 4 days.

*Note: Some cake ingredients are sensitive to heat. If you find that the mousse or chocolate-coconut frosting is getting too warm when assembling the cake, simply refrigerate them for 15 to 20 minutes, until they are stiff and easier to work with.

Fall Months

Fall is the season when the rhythms of life are enjoyed at a slower, steadier pace. As the days grow shorter we're more inclined to slowly peel off the covers in the morning, or take joy in turning on the oven once again and baking a morning treat. There's a distinct autumnal scent in the air, crisp and dewy, with an earthy fragrance of freshly fallen leaves. It's also a time of harvest, when the produce around us shows up in beautiful hues of deep green, golden yellow, and burnt orange. I love taking trips to the market on cool mornings with a cup of coffee in hand to take in the aisles of crisp New York apples and the aroma of hot apple cider and cinnamon doughnuts wafting in the air, all while observing knobby winter squash, juicy pears, and red grapes. Fall is the last hurrah before we hibernate for the winter months.

French Toast with Grape Compote ⓥ

MAKES: 6 PIECES OF TOAST // **PREP TIME:** 15 MINUTES // **COOK TIME:** 40 MINUTES

Chickpea flour makes a great batter for French toast, one that mimics the original almost completely. The batter is thinner than a traditional egg-based batter, but coats and adheres to the bread perfectly, and provides the center of the bread with that custard-like texture we all know and love. October is the grape season, where we get our choice of the freshest, juiciest little spheres. Any red grape will work beautifully for the compote—just make sure they are seedless.

1 cup (120 g) chickpea flour

¼ cup (30 g) plus 1 teaspoon arrowroot powder

½ teaspoon ground cinnamon

Pinch of salt

1 cup (240 ml) plus 2 tablespoons almond milk

½ teaspoon pure vanilla extract

2 tablespoons coconut oil

6 slices bread of choice

2 cups (170 g) seedless red grapes of choice

2 tablespoons maple syrup

2 teaspoons lemon juice

Chopped hazelnuts

❶ In a shallow bowl, whisk together the flour, ¼ cup arrowroot, cinnamon, and salt. Whisk in the milk and vanilla until no lumps remain. Set aside and let the batter rest.

❷ Turn oven to 200°F (95°C) and place a parchment paper–lined baking sheet inside.

❸ Heat a 10- to 12-inch skillet over medium heat. Test the pan by spritzing it with water: if the water sizzles and evaporates the pan is ready. Add 1 tablespoon of oil to the pan. Dunk the bread quickly into the batter, coating both sides. Transfer the bread to the skillet and cook for 3 to 4 minutes on both sides, until browned and crisp. Transfer to the warm oven and repeat with the remaining slices, using the additional 1 tablespoon of oil as needed for cooking the remaining slices. You can cook more than one slice at a time, but be careful not to overcrowd the skillet.

❹ For the compote, bring the grapes, syrup, and lemon juice to a simmer over medium-low heat. Cook the mixture for 8 to 10 minutes, until the grapes have burst a bit and the mixture is thick and syrupy.

❺ Plate the French toast and top with hot grape compote and chopped hazelnuts.

Carrot Cake Breakfast Cookies

MAKES: ELEVEN 3-INCH COOKIES // **PREP TIME:** 15 MINUTES // **COOK TIME:** 18 TO 20 MINUTES

The autumnal months bring about not only a change in food but also its flavors. We incorporate more warming spices, bake more often, and use up the abundance of root vegetables coming our way. Cookies are one of those things I wish I could eat every single morning. I prefer a sweet breakfast but don't like the effects that eating sweets in the morning has on me. That's why breakfast cookies are so great—they combine everything that's super about cookies and make them a bit more nourishing to get your day started off right. These cookies are hearty but still cookie-like, and full of those warming spices we know and love from a traditional carrot cake.

¾ cup (90 g) chickpea flour

¾ cup (79 g) gluten-free old-fashioned rolled oats

½ cup (10 g) puffed brown rice

1 teaspoon ground cinnamon

½ teaspoon baking soda

½ teaspoon sea salt

½ teaspoon ground ginger

½ teaspoon ground nutmeg

1 cup (86 g) grated carrots (roughly 2 large carrots)

1 large egg

½ cup (66 g) chopped hazelnuts

⅓ cup (80 ml) maple syrup

¼ cup (60 ml) coconut oil, melted

½ cup (120 g) almond butter

1 teaspoon pure vanilla extract

❶ Preheat oven to 350°F (180°C) and line two baking sheets with parchment paper. Set aside.

❷ In a large bowl, whisk together the flour, oats, rice, cinnamon, baking soda, salt, ginger, and nutmeg. Set aside. In another large bowl, whisk together the grated carrots, egg, hazelnuts, syrup, oil, almond butter, and vanilla. Using a rubber spatula, mix the dry ingredients into the wet mixture and mix until thoroughly combined.

❸ Using a standard ice-cream scoop, scoop the mixture out onto the baking sheets (about 2 heaping tablespoons), leaving 2 inches between cookies.

❹ Bake for 18 to 20 minutes, rotating the cookie sheets halfway through, until lightly browned and golden. Let the cookies cool completely before serving. Cookies can be stored in an airtight container at room temperature for 3 days.

Chickpea Omelet
with Shiitakes and Microgreens ⓥ

MAKES: 5 TO 6 OMELETS // **PREP TIME:** 20 MINUTES // **COOK TIME:** 20 MINUTES

Omelets of any kind have an inherent easiness about them and can be filled with whatever you desire. This chickpea flour–based omelet has a very similar texture and consistency to an egg-based omelet but cooks up faster, and you never have to worry about it being undercooked. The flaxseed meal and chickpea flour come together to form an egg replacer while also providing a flavorful substitute.

1 tablespoon ground flaxseed meal

1 cup (240 ml) plus 3 tablespoons water

1 cup (120 g) chickpea flour

½ teaspoon sea salt, plus more to taste

⅛ teaspoon freshly ground pepper, plus more to taste

½ teaspoon rice wine vinegar

2 teaspoons extra virgin olive oil

1 teaspoon toasted sesame oil

2 bunches scallions, ends trimmed and white and light green parts sliced thin

2 dozen shiitake mushrooms (200 g), stems removed and sliced thin

1 cup (20 g) microgreens

❶ In a small bowl, whisk together the flaxseed and 3 tablespoons of water; set aside for 10 minutes to thicken. In a medium bowl, whisk together the flour, salt, and pepper; add the remaining water and vinegar, and stir until no lumps remain. Mix in the flax mixture and set aside.

❷ Heat 1 teaspoon of olive oil and the sesame oil in a skillet over medium heat. Once hot, add the sliced scallions; cook until soft and transparent, about 1 minute. Add the mushrooms and season with salt and pepper; stir and cook for 5 to 6 minutes, until tender. Remove from the heat and set aside.

❸ Cook the omelets. Heat a skillet over medium heat; once hot, add about 1 teaspoon of oil, enough to lightly cover the bottom of the pan. Using a ¼-cup measure, pour the batter into the pan, swirling to cover the bottom. Let the omelet cook for 1 to 2 minutes, until you see bubbles appear in the center and on the sides. Flip the omelet over and cook for another 30 seconds to 1 minute, until lightly browned. Remove from the heat and place the omelet on a large plate and keep warm with a dish towel. Repeat with the remaining batter, adding more oil as needed.

❹ Divide the cooked mushrooms and microgreens among the omelets, reserving some microgreens. Fold one side of the omelet over. Garnish with leftover microgreens.

Chickpea Tzatziki Dip ⓥ

MAKES: ROUGHLY 1½ CUPS // **SERVES:** 4 TO 6 // **PREP TIME:** 12 HOURS // **COOK TIME:** 4 HOURS

Tzatziki is a Greek yogurt–based sauce and dip. It's served cold and is flavored with cooling cucumbers, garlic, and lemon juice. Chickpea flour is used here to form that creamy base that tzatziki is known for without the yogurt and does a remarkable job of duplicating it entirely. This is best made the day before you plan to serve it, but can also be made the morning of; it needs time to cool and for the flavors to meld. This dip is great to serve alongside chickpea flatbread for dipping (see Flatbread with Harissa, Kale, and Gaeta Olives, page 39), olives, and a big salad.

1 medium cucumber, grated with a box grater

1 cup (240 ml) water

¼ cup (30 g) chickpea flour

¼ cup (45 g) raw cashews, soaked overnight and drained

2 garlic cloves, roughly chopped

1 tablespoon apple cider vinegar

1 tablespoon extra virgin olive oil

1 tablespoon lemon juice

Coarse sea salt and freshly ground pepper

2 tablespoons chopped dill

❶ Place the grated cucumber in a fine-mesh sieve. Use your palm and push to squeeze out as much liquid as possible; set aside.

❷ In a small saucepan, whisk together the water and flour until smooth. Turn heat to medium and continue whisking until the mixture thickens, about 6 to 7 minutes; the mixture will resemble a roux or melted cheese. Remove from the heat.

❸ Place the flour mixture, cashews, garlic, vinegar, oil, lemon juice, and salt and pepper, to taste, in a high-speed blender; blend for 1 minute, until smooth. Pour the mixture into a bowl; stir in the grated cucumber and dill. Let the tzatziki come to room temperature, then refrigerate for at least 4 hours.

❹ Remove from the refrigerator when ready to serve and give it a good stir.

Baked Buttermilk Onion Rings ⓥ

SERVES: 2 TO 4 AS A SIDE OR SNACK // **PREP TIME:** 4 HOURS 10 MINUTES // **COOK TIME:** 20 MINUTES

I have to say, I have pretty bad memories of onion rings. I never really enjoyed biting into greasy batter only to find that the onion center was basically raw. I stayed away from them for most of my life, until I became curious about making them the way I envisioned: crunchy on the outside and tender on the inside. It wasn't until I started making homemade onion rings that I truly enjoyed them. I've found that the secret to getting the onion center tender is to soak them overnight (or at least for a few hours) in an almond milk and vinegar "buttermilk." Then, they're lightly battered using cornmeal, bread crumbs (for that undeniable crunch we all think of when we think onion rings), and chickpea flour, which gives the rings a nutty flavor you don't get with other flours. Serve these beside your favorite dinner or as a snack with some dip.

1 cup (240 ml) almond milk

1 tablespoon apple cider vinegar

1½ teaspoons sea salt

Freshly ground pepper

1 large onion, cut into ½-inch rings

½ cup (80 g) gluten-free bread crumbs

½ cup (60 g) chickpea flour

½ cup (66 g) stone-ground cornmeal

2 teaspoons sesame seeds

1 teaspoon garlic powder

1 teaspoon dried parsley

1 Whisk together the milk and vinegar; let mixture sit for 5 minutes. Then whisk in ½ teaspoon of salt and pepper, to taste. Place the sliced onion rings in a shallow baking dish and pour the mixture over top so all the onion slices are submerged. Cover with plastic wrap and refrigerate for at least 4 hours or overnight.

2 When ready to cook, remove the onions from the refrigerator and set aside. Preheat oven to 450°F (230°C) and line a baking sheet with parchment paper. Set aside.

3 In a shallow bowl or pie dish, combine the bread crumbs, flour, cornmeal, sesame seeds, garlic powder, parsley, and 1 teaspoon salt.

4 One at a time, use your fingers to press the onions into the cornmeal and flour mixture, and then lay them onto the prepared baking sheet. Repeat with the remaining onions.

5 Bake the onion rings 7 to 10 minutes. Remove the pan and flip the rings over; bake for another 7 to 10 minutes on the other side, until lightly brown and crisp. Serve immediately while hot.

Savory Crepes with Beet Pâté

MAKES: 11 TO 12 SIX-INCH CREPES // **SERVES:** 4 AS A SIDE OR AN APPETIZER
PREP TIME: 1 HOUR 30 MINUTES // **COOK TIME:** 15 TO 20 MINUTES

Whether you're stuffing crepes with beans or legumes, topping them with a salad, serving them alongside a soup, or using them as an alternative to crackers or bread, they always serve a necessary purpose. A lot of times my husband and I opt for a less-structured dinner of a large salad, perhaps some homemade sweet potato fries, and some iteration of chips and dip. We began using fresh crepes instead of crackers or chips and always pair them with a beet hummus or lentil dip. We found that the warm crepes were just the thing a cool dip needs this time of year.

PÂTÉ

1 bunch beets (roughly 3 medium beets)

2 tablespoons extra virgin olive oil, plus oil to coat beets

1 small shallot, roughly chopped

1 garlic clove, roughly chopped

2 tablespoons walnuts

2 teaspoons lemon juice

2 teaspoons sherry vinegar

1½ teaspoons nutritional yeast

1 teaspoon toasted coriander seeds

1 teaspoon Dijon mustard

½ teaspoon sea salt

Freshly ground pepper

CREPES

1 cup (240 ml) almond milk

1 cup (120 g) chickpea flour

2 large eggs

2 tablespoons plus 1 teaspoon extra virgin olive oil

2 teaspoons chopped chives

1 teaspoon poppy seeds

¼ teaspoon sea salt

½ cup (30 g) chopped parsley

❶ Preheat oven to 400°F (200°C). Trim the roots and tips from the beets; wash and pat dry. Tear a large piece of foil, place the beets in the center, and drizzle with oil to coat. Bring the sides up and over the beets to make a loose packet. Cook the beets for 45 minutes to 1 hour, until a sharp knife is easily inserted into the center of the beets. Set aside and allow to cool.

❷ Slip off the beet skins with your fingers and discard. Roughly chop the beets. Combine the beets, shallot, garlic, 2 tablespoons of oil, walnuts, lemon juice, vinegar, yeast, coriander, mustard, salt, and pepper, to taste, in an upright blender or food processor; blend for 1 minute, scraping down the sides as you go along until you have a smooth mixture. Taste and adjust any seasonings, if needed. Scrape into a bowl, cover with plastic wrap, and refrigerate until ready to use.

❸ In a large bowl, whisk together the milk, flour, eggs, 2 tablespoons of oil, chives, poppy seeds, and salt, until thoroughly combined. Transfer to a bowl and cover loosely with plastic wrap; place in the refrigerator for at least 30 minutes or overnight.

❹ Heat a large skillet over medium heat; test the pan with a splash of water: if it sizzles and evaporates, the pan is ready. Add 1 teaspoon of oil to the pan, or enough to coat the bottom; scoop a scant ¼ cup of batter into the hot skillet; swirl the pan to evenly distribute the batter. Cook until bubbles form on the outside and middle of the crepe, about 1 minute; carefully flip the crepe over and cook for an additional 30 seconds, until lightly golden. Repeat with the remaining batter, stacking the crepes on top of each other on a plate as you go along.

❺ Remove the beet pâté from the refrigerator and serve with warm crepes, and garnish with parsley.

Spaghetti Squash Fritters

MAKES: 10 CAKES **//** **SERVES:** 5 **//** **PREP TIME:** 45 MINUTES **//** **COOK TIME:** 20 MINUTES

Winter squashes are perhaps the most ubiquitous vegetables in many fall and winter meals, partly because there are so many varieties, but also because of their various flavors and textures. I'm partial to spaghetti squash, though—its unique strands of flesh that resemble spaghetti are what appealed to me from the first time I ate one. The strands make a perfect base for this fritter, giving it flavor and texture all in one bite. The chickpea flour is toasted, lending a delicious, nutty flavor. I love making these fritters ahead of time, refrigerating them, and then heating them up throughout the week.

⅓ cup (40 g) chickpea flour

1 medium spaghetti squash, halved lengthwise

¼ cup extra virgin olive oil, plus extra for rub

1 cup (67 g) chopped collard greens

¼ cup (15 g) chopped parsley

1 small red onion

2 garlic cloves, minced

1 large egg, whisked

1 tablespoon ground flaxseed meal

½ teaspoon baking powder

½ teaspoon chili powder

½ teaspoon sea salt

1 teaspoon ground cumin

Chickpea Sour Cream (page 152)

Microgreens

❶ Heat a skillet over medium heat. Once hot, add the flour and stir; toast until golden and fragrant, about 7 to 8 minutes. Remove from the skillet and place in a mixing bowl.

❷ Preheat oven to 400°F (200°C) and line a baking sheet with parchment paper; set aside.

❸ Scrape the seeds from the squash and rub the exposed flesh lightly with oil. Place each half with the cut side down on the baking sheet and bake for 35 to 40 minutes, until a knife inserted can be removed easily. Let the squash cool. One half at a time, use a fork to scrape the squash strings and wring them out with a cheesecloth or clean dish towel, removing as much liquid as you can. Place in a large bowl and repeat with the other half.

❹ Add the collards, parsley, onion, and garlic to the bowl and mix. Add the whisked egg and toss everything to coat. Set aside.

❺ In another bowl, combine the toasted flour, flaxseed meal, baking powder, chili powder, salt, and cumin. Add this dry mixture to the vegetable mixture and combine thoroughly.

❻ Heat 2 tablespoons of oil in a skillet over medium heat until hot and shimmering. In batches, scoop roughly 2 tablespoons of squash mixture into the skillet; flatten with the back of a spatula or spoon. Cook for 4 to 5 minutes, until golden brown and crisp; flip over and cook for another 2 minutes. Remove from the pan with a slotted spatula and place on a paper towel–lined plate. Repeat with remaining mixture, adding the remaining oil as needed.

❼ Serve the fritters warm with sour cream and microgreens. Fritters can be refrigerated in an airtight container for up to 3 days.

Beetballs with Rosemary White Bean Cream

MAKES: 16 BEETBALLS // **SERVES:** 4 // **PREP TIME:** 1 HOUR 15 MINUTES // **COOK TIME:** 15 TO 20 MINUTES

These are by far a favorite recipe in my house. Growing up in a part-Italian household, my family was always serving up a large bowl of spaghetti with homemade meatballs and red sauce. My parents would serve the dish with a good portion of Reggiano cheese. While I wouldn't dream of trying to re-create a meatless version of those childhood meatballs, I did make a riff on them here, incorporating some of the spices and herbs my mom would use to make them super flavorful. And while a red sauce would do just fine, I really love how the white bean cream makes the dish a bit lighter.

BEETBALLS

1 large or 2 small golden beets

1 tablespoon extra virgin olive oil, plus extra for baking and brushing

½ cup (60 g) chickpea flour

½ teaspoon fennel seeds

¼ teaspoon cumin seeds

¼ cup (35 g) toasted sunflower seeds

1 small yellow onion, chopped

3 garlic cloves, roughly chopped

1½ cups (190 g) cooked quinoa

1 tablespoon ground flaxseed meal

1 tablespoon tomato paste

2 large eggs

1 teaspoon sea salt

½ teaspoon red pepper flakes

2 teaspoons chopped thyme (or 1 teaspoon dry)

2 teaspoons chopped oregano (or 1 teaspoon dry)

¼ cup (15 g) chopped parsley

BEAN CREAM

One 15-ounce (425 g) can organic cannellini beans, drained and rinsed

2 large garlic cloves, chopped

2 tablespoons extra virgin olive oil

1½ teaspoons lemon juice

1 tablespoon nutritional yeast

1½ teaspoons apple cider vinegar

¾ teaspoon sea salt

1 tablespoon chopped rosemary

❶ Preheat oven to 400°F (200°C) and trim the root and tip of the beet(s). Rinse and pat dry. Place the beet(s) in a piece of foil, drizzle with oil, and place in a small baking dish. Cook for roughly 45 minutes to 1 hour, until a knife inserted can be removed easily. Set aside and let cool. Rub the skin from the beet(s) and discard; rinse and pat dry. Cut the beet(s) into rough chunks and set aside.

❷ Heat a skillet over medium heat; add the flour and stir; toast for 7 to 8 minutes, until fragrant and lightly browned. Remove from the skillet and let cool. Set aside.

❸ Heat the same skillet over medium-low and add the fennel and cumin seeds; toast for 2 to 3 minutes, stirring every so often, until toasted and fragrant. Remove from the skillet and let cool. Place the seeds in a mortar or in a spice grinder and grind well. Set aside.

❹ Toast the sunflower seeds in the skillet over medium-low heat for 3 minutes, until toasted and golden. Set aside and let cool.

❺ Heat 1 tablespoon of oil in a large skillet over medium heat; once the pan is hot, add the onion; cook until soft and translucent, about 3 minutes. Add the garlic and stir; cook until fragrant, about 30 to 40 seconds. Remove the pan from the heat and set aside.

❻ Preheat oven to 350°F (180°C) and line two baking sheets with parchment paper; set aside.

❼ In a food processor fitted with a metal S blade, combine the baked beet, ground cumin and fennel, toasted sunflower seeds, sautéed onion and garlic, quinoa, flaxseed meal, tomato paste, eggs, salt, and chili flakes. Pulse to combine, until the mixture is blended; transfer to a large bowl and fold in the toasted flour and herbs. Refrigerate for 1 hour.

❽ Pinch off tablespoon-size pieces of the mixture and roll between your palms; place on the prepared baking sheets, brush the beetballs lightly with olive oil, and bake for 15 to 20 minutes, until golden brown.

9 While the beetballs are baking, make the sauce. In an upright high-speed blender, combine the beans, garlic, oil, lemon juice, yeast, vinegar, and salt; blend on high for 1 minute, scraping down the sides as needed. Transfer the sauce to a small saucepan, stir in the rosemary, and turn the heat to medium-low, stirring every few minutes until steaming and hot.

10 Plate the beetballs and drizzle with warm sauce over top.

Chai-Spice Swirl Breakfast Bread

MAKES: ONE 8-INCH ROUND CAKE // **SERVES:** 8 // **PREP TIME:** 15 MINUTES

COOK TIME: 35 TO 40 MINUTES

This breakfast treat is perfect to serve with a hot pot of coffee on a cool morning. It's rich and velvety, and is riddled with a chai-spice and muscovado swirl right through the center that echoes a traditional coffee cake or cinnamon swirl. I call for muscovado sugar, an unrefined sugar that contains a large quantity of molasses, giving the swirl an undeniable richness. If you can't find muscovado or don't want to purchase it, it can be substituted with brown sugar or even coconut sugar.

¼ cup (30 g) muscovado sugar

¼ cup (35 g) pine nuts

1 teaspoon ground cinnamon

1 teaspoon ground ginger

½ teaspoon ground nutmeg

¼ teaspoon ground cardamom

¼ teaspoon ground allspice

1 cup (120 g) chickpea flour

½ cup (57 g) oat flour

¼ cup (30 g) arrowroot powder

1 teaspoon baking powder

1 teaspoon psyllium husk powder

½ teaspoon baking soda

½ teaspoon sea salt

1 cup (220 g) pumpkin puree

⅔ cup (96 g) coconut sugar

2 large eggs

½ cup (120 ml) coconut milk

½ cup (120 ml) coconut oil, melted

1½ teaspoons pure vanilla extract

❶ Preheat oven to 350°F (180°C); grease an 8-inch tube pan and set aside.

❷ Make the swirl filling. Whisk together the muscovado sugar, pine nuts, and spices; set aside.

❸ In a large bowl, whisk together the flours, arrowroot, baking powder, psyllium husk, baking soda, and salt. In another large bowl, whisk together the pumpkin puree, coconut sugar, eggs, milk, oil, and vanilla. In batches, add the dry ingredients to the wet and combine thoroughly with a rubber spatula.

❹ Pour half the batter into the pan; evenly sprinkle the swirl filling over top, then pour the remaining batter evenly into the pan, using a spatula to level the top.

❺ Bake for 35 to 40 minutes, until a cake tester inserted into the center comes out clean. Remove from the heat and let cool completely before inverting the cake to remove from the pan and slicing.

Apple Crumb Bars ⓥ

MAKES: 16 BARS // **PREP TIME:** 35 MINUTES // **COOK TIME:** 40 TO 45 MINUTES

These apple crumb bars are essentially an apple pie with crumb topping in handheld form, which makes them even more fun to eat if you ask me! While you can certainly serve them at room temperature, I recommend heating them before serving, for optimal deliciousness. I suggest using an 8 x 8-inch pan with a removable bottom because these bars are delicate and a removable bottom makes lifting them from the pan easier. However, you could just as easily line an 8 x 8-inch pan with a piece of parchment paper hanging over the sides of the pan, giving you "wings" to lift the bars out.

CRUMBLE

¾ cup (79 g) gluten-free old-fashioned rolled oats

½ cup (55 g) sorghum flour

½ teaspoon ground cinnamon

¼ teaspoon ground ginger

¼ teaspoon sea salt

¼ cup (60 ml) coconut oil, melted

1 tablespoon plus 1 teaspoon maple syrup

FILLING

6 medium apples, peeled and cored (Gala or Pink Lady preferred)

½ cup (72 g) coconut sugar

1 tablespoon arrowroot powder

½ teaspoon ground cinnamon

½ teaspoon ground nutmeg

¼ teaspoon sea salt

1 tablespoon coconut oil

CRUST

1 cup (105 g) gluten-free old-fashioned rolled oats

¾ cup (90 g) chickpea flour

½ cup (70 g) hazelnuts

¼ teaspoon sea salt

1/4 cup plus 2 tablespoons coconut oil, melted

2 tablespoons maple syrup

❶ Preheat oven to 350°F (180°C) and grease the bottom and sides of an 8 x 8-inch square pan with a removable bottom. (Or, line the pan with parchment paper as described in the headnote.)

❷ Make the crumb topping. In a bowl, whisk together the oats, flour, spices, and salt. Pour in the oil and syrup; use a spatula to mix evenly. Cover with plastic wrap and place in the refrigerator until ready to use.

❸ Make the filling, slice the apples thin, about ⅛-inch in thickness, and place in a large bowl. Add the sugar, arrowroot, spices, and salt; stir and thoroughly combine.

❹ Heat the oil in a large pan with at least 2-inch sides over medium heat. When the pan is hot, add the apple mixture, stirring every few seconds, until the apples are tender and soft and the liquids are caramelized; about 10 to 12 minutes (cook time may depend on the size of your pan—the larger the pan the less time it will take). Remove the pan from heat and set aside.

❺ Make the crust. In a large bowl, whisk together the dry ingredients. Pour in the oil and syrup until thoroughly combined. Dough should hold together when you pinch it between your fingers.

❻ Place the crust dough in your prepared pan; use your fingers to distribute evenly into the bottom and corners of the pan. Prick the dough all over with a fork; bake for 5 to 7 minutes, until the edges are golden.

❼ Add apples to the parbaked crust, arranging them in an even layer, and distribute the crumble over the top of the apples. Bake for 30 to 35 minutes, until golden brown (if you notice your topping is browning too quickly, place a loose-fitting piece of foil over the pan for the duration of the bake time).

❽ Remove the pan from the oven and let cool completely. Use a thin knife to loosen the edges from the pan, carefully push the bottom of the pan out from the sides, and place on a large plate or platter. Using a sharp knife, and slice into sixteen squares. Bars can be stored at room temperature for up to 3 days.

Buttermilk Chickpea Corn Bread

MAKES: ONE 10-INCH ROUND OF CORN BREAD // **SERVES:** 8 // **PREP TIME:** 20 MINUTES
COOK TIME: 25 TO 30 MINUTES

Corn bread is one of those nostalgic items found on most tables this time of year. This version is a far more savory rendition than the one I grew up eating; it's made with cultured coconut milk, giving the bread a tart, moist flavor and texture. The chickpea flour and olive oil also help to make this a great incarnation of a traditional corn bread.

1½ cups (350 ml) coconut milk

1 tablespoon plus 1 teaspoon apple cider vinegar

1 cup (120 g) chickpea flour

1 cup (134 g) cornmeal

1 teaspoon sea salt

1 teaspoon baking powder

½ teaspoon baking soda

2 large eggs

¼ cup extra virgin olive oil

1 Preheat oven to 375°F (190°C) and grease a 10-inch oven-safe skillet; set aside.

2 In a liquid measure, whisk together the milk and vinegar; set aside.

3 In a bowl, whisk together the flour, cornmeal, salt, baking powder, and baking soda.

4 Whisk the egg and oil into the milk mixture until pale yellow, and then mix into the dry ingredients with a rubber spatula until thoroughly incorporated and smooth.

5 Pour the batter into the skillet; bake for 25 to 30 minutes, until golden.

6 Let the corn bread cool for 20 minutes before serving. Corn bread can be stored in an airtight container at room temperature for up to 2 days—corn bread will get increasingly dry each day.

Herbed Sweet Potato Biscuits Ⓥ

MAKES: SIX 2-INCH BISCUITS // **PREP TIME:** 10 MINUTES // **COOK TIME:** 13 TO 15 MINUTES

These sweet potato biscuits are hearty and rich with a velvety texture. They're perfect to accompany a holiday meal or as a savory morning baked good. The sweet potato makes these sweeter and a bit more dense than a conventional biscuit, but tender and flaky all the same. These are perfect to accompany any meal as a side, but they also make for a fun main dish. I like to toast them and serve sloppy joe–style with vegetarian chili or fill them and make a sandwich.

1 cup (120 g) chickpea flour

½ cup (55 g) sorghum flour, plus extra for dusting

½ cup (60 g) arrowroot powder

1 tablespoon cane sugar

1 teaspoon baking powder

½ teaspoon baking soda

½ teaspoon sea salt

¾ cup (175 g) cooked and mashed sweet potato*

¼ cup (60 ml) almond milk, plus more for brushing

¼ cup (60 ml) extra virgin olive oil

1 teaspoon apple cider vinegar

1 tablespoon fresh thyme, plus more for topping

1 large egg, whisked (optional)**

❶ Preheat oven to 425°F (220°C) and line a baking sheet with parchment paper; set aside.

❷ In a bowl, whisk together the flours, arrowroot, sugar, baking powder, baking soda, and salt. In another bowl, whisk together the sweet potato, milk, oil, and vinegar. Add the potato mixture and the thyme to the dry ingredients, and fold ingredients together with a rubber spatula until the mixture is combined. Sprinkle the parchment-lined baking sheet with sorghum flour and turn the dough out onto it; knead with your hands until the dough comes together.

❸ Flatten the dough into a 1-inch rectangle; if the dough seems sticky, dust with more flour. Using a 2-inch biscuit cutter, punch out 6 biscuits, rerolling the dough as you go.

❹ If using the egg wash, brush the tops and sides of the biscuits with it and top with the leftover thyme leaves. If you are not using the egg wash, brush tops and sides lightly with milk and top with leftover thyme. Bake for 13 to 15 minutes, rotating halfway through, until golden brown.

❺ Let the biscuits cool for 5 to 10 minutes; serve warm.

*Note: To bake the potato, preheat oven to 400°F (200°C); line a baking sheet with parchment or foil. Bake for 45 to 50 minutes, until tender. Remove from the oven, slice in half, and let cool completely.

**Note: The egg wash gives the biscuits a nice color when baked; however, leaving it out doesn't change the taste of the biscuit.

Root Vegetable Crumble ⓥ

SERVES: 6 AS A SIDE // **PREP TIME:** 35 MINUTES // **COOK TIME:** 45 TO 50 MINUTES

This is by far one of my favorite recipes to serve as a side for the Thanksgiving holiday or for a casual gathering of friends or family. It's one of those one-pot dishes that serves an entire room of hungry people. This crumble is a great twist on a dessert crumble—by adding tons of savory notes, plenty of root vegetables, and some hearty herbs, this dish is transformed from a dessert into a hearty meal.

CRUMBLE TOPPING

1 cup (105 g) gluten-free old-fashioned rolled oats

½ cup (60 g) chickpea flour

⅓ cup (33 g) chopped walnuts

2 tablespoons hemp seeds

1 teaspoon garlic powder

1 teaspoon chopped rosemary

½ teaspoon sea salt

Freshly ground pepper

¼ cup plus 1 to 2 tablespoons extra virgin olive oil

FILLING

1 sweet potato, peeled and sliced in half and cut into 1-inch pieces

2 turnips, peeled and cut into ½-inch pieces

2 carrots, cut into ½-inch pieces

2 shallots, diced

2 garlic cloves, minced

2 teaspoons quality Dijon mustard (preferably Maille)

2 tablespoons plus 1½ teaspoons extra virgin olive oil

¾ teaspoon sea salt

Freshly ground pepper

1 sprig of sage, stem discarded and leaves finely chopped

❶ Make the crumble topping. In a large bowl, whisk together the oats, flour, walnuts, hemp seeds, garlic powder, rosemary, salt, and pepper, to taste. Mix in ¼ cup plus 1 tablespoon of oil with a fork until the mixture resemble coarse crumbs; if the mixture is still a bit dry, add the remaining tablespoon of oil. Cover with plastic wrap and place in the refrigerator until ready to use.

❷ Preheat oven to 375°F (190°C) and grease a 9-inch baking dish; set aside.

❸ Prepare the filling. Place the potato, turnips, carrots, shallots, and garlic in a large bowl. Mix in the mustard, oil, salt, and pepper, to taste. Fold in the sage and then transfer the vegetables to the prepared baking dish. Remove the crumble from the refrigerator. Use your fingers to break up any large clumps and distribute evenly over the top of the vegetables.

❹ Bake for 45 to 50 minutes, until the crumble is browned and the vegetables are tender. If the crumble topping is browning too much, cover with a piece of loose-fitting foil for the remaining time. Serve warm.

Moroccan-Spiced Lentil and Pumpkin Burgers

MAKES: 4 PATTIES // **PREP TIME:** 1 HOUR 30 MINUTES // **COOK TIME:** 45 TO 50 MINUTES

These burgers are a really tasty take on a traditional vegetable burger, incorporating many of the warm spices that are usually found in Moroccan fare, such as cinnamon, turmeric, and coriander. The harissa mayo stands up well to the hearty burger patty with its spice and tang, while the crispy and crunchy shallots add some conventionality. I also like eating these burgers as salad toppers or to crumble up in a tortilla with greens.

PATTIES

1½ cups (360 ml) water

½ cup (100 g) dry lentils (beluga or brown), rinsed and picked over

¾ teaspoon sea salt, plus more to taste

1 tablespoon extra virgin olive oil, plus extra for brushing

1 small onion, diced

2 garlic cloves, minced

One 1-inch piece of ginger, minced

½ cup (110 g) pumpkin puree

1 large egg

½ cup (60 g) chickpea flour, toasted

1 tablespoon dried parsley

1 teaspoon ground cinnamon

1 teaspoon ground coriander

1 teaspoon ground cumin

½ teaspoon ground turmeric

Freshly ground pepper

TOPPINGS

1 tablespoon extra virgin olive oil

3 shallots, sliced thin

½ cup Vegenaise (or mayonnaise)

1 tablespoon harissa paste

1 head leafy lettuce (about 480 g)

Gluten-free hamburger buns

1. Bring the water, lentils, and a pinch of salt to a boil, then turn the heat down to a gentle simmer. Cook uncovered for 15 to 20 minutes. Start tasting the lentils after 15 minutes, testing to see if the lentils are tender. Once cooked through, remove from the heat and drain off any remaining water. Lay out the lentils to towel-dry and cool.

2. Heat enough oil to coat the bottom of a large skillet (about 1 tablespoon) over medium heat; once the pan is hot, add the onion and cook until soft and translucent, about 3 minutes. Add the garlic and ginger; stir and cook for another 30 to 40 seconds. Remove from heat and let cool. (Reserve the skillet for later.)

3. Add the cooled lentils, pumpkin puree, onion, garlic, and ginger to a food processor and pulse until chunky. Transfer the mixture to a large bowl and fold in the egg and mix until combined. Add the flour, parsley, spices, ¾ teaspoon of salt, and pepper, to taste, and stir until combined.

4. Cover the bowl with plastic wrap and refrigerate for 1 hour or overnight.

5. Preheat oven to 350°F (180°C). Line a baking sheet with parchment paper and brush with a thin layer of olive oil; set aside.

6. Form mixture into 3-inch round patties with ½-inch thickness, and place onto the baking sheet.

7. Bake for 15 minutes, until the bottoms are lightly golden. Gently flip the patties over; bake for another 15 to 20 minutes, until golden brown.

8. Make the frizzled shallots. In a skillet, heat the oil over medium; once the oil is hot, add the shallots and cook for about 10 minutes, stirring every so often until the shallots are golden and crisp. Transfer the shallots to a paper towel–lined plate; set aside.

9. In a small bowl, whisk together the Vegenaise (or mayonnaise) and harissa until combined; set aside.

10. Toast the buns and spread the harissa mayo on each side. Divide the lettuce between the burgers as a topping; add a patty and the frizzled shallots.

Chili-Roasted Pumpkin
with Chickpea-Miso Gravy Ⓥ

SERVES: 8 // **PREP TIME:** 25 MINUTES // **COOK TIME:** 40 TO 45 MINUTES

Gravy is a big deal around this time of year, gracing the tables of so many across the country. I never really understood the allure of gravy, since it always made whatever I was eating that much heavier. This chickpea flour–based gravy adds density without the heaviness and has an amazing umami flavor thanks to the miso. I like a bit of pep, courtesy of the sriracha in this dish, but if you're not a fan of much spice, I indicate using chili powder instead.

PUMPKIN

1 small pumpkin (roughly 3 pounds/1,360 g)

1 tablespoon extra virgin olive oil

1 teaspoon rice vinegar

1 teaspoon toasted sesame oil

1 teaspoon sriracha (or chili powder)

Coarse sea salt

QUINOA

2 cups (480 ml) water

1 cup (190 g) black quinoa

Fine sea salt

¼ cup (15 g) chopped cilantro

⅓ cup (50 g) pomegranate seeds

1 bunch scallions, ends trimmed and thinly sliced

GRAVY

1 tablespoon plus 2 teaspoons extra virgin olive oil

1 shallot, chopped

1 garlic clove, chopped

2 cups (480 ml) low-sodium vegetable broth

½ cup (60 g) chickpea flour

2 tablespoons gluten-free mellow white miso

2 tablespoons toasted sesame seeds

❶ Preheat oven to 400°F (200°C) and line a baking sheet with parchment. Slice the pumpkin in half, and then slice each half into four even pieces.

❷ Whisk together the olive oil, vinegar, sesame oil, sriracha, and a big pinch of coarse salt. Brush the pumpkin pieces with the sriracha mixture and bake cut-side up for 40 to 45 minutes, until tender and the edges are golden brown. Set aside.

❸ Make the quinoa. Add the water, quinoa, and a big pinch of salt to a lidded pot. Bring to a boil, cover, and reduce the heat; simmer for 15 to 20 minutes, until the quinoa is cooked and the water is absorbed. Let the quinoa rest for 10 minutes, then transfer to a large bowl and mix in the cilantro, pomegranate seeds, and scallions.

❹ In the last 10 minutes of the pumpkin cooking, make the gravy. Heat 2 teaspoons of olive oil in a skillet over medium heat, add the shallot and stir, and cook until translucent and soft. Stir in the garlic and cook for 30 to 40 seconds, until fragrant. Remove the pan from the heat.

❺ In an upright blender, blend together the cooked onion and garlic, broth, flour, miso, and the remaining 1 tablespoon of olive oil. Pour into a large saucepan over medium heat. Stir until the consistency thickens, about 10 minutes. Turn the heat to low and stir every few minutes.

❻ Plate the pumpkin, spoon the quinoa mixture over top, and drizzle with gravy and sesame seeds.

Squash Doughnuts
with Almond-Butter Glaze

MAKES: 10 DOUGHNUTS // **PREP TIME:** 10 MINUTES // **COOK TIME:** 13 TO 15 MINUTES

I'm pretty sure we all have apple-cider-doughnut or sugar-doughnut nostalgia from when we were little. There was a small family-run farm near where I grew up that would make their own fried doughnuts each weekend morning for the entirety of the fall season. When that farm was sold, we were left with a chain-run doughnut shop that just didn't stand up. Years later, when I was shopping for kitchen supplies, I was thrilled to find doughnut pans to make homemade, baked doughnuts. The baked variety of homemade doughnuts are an easy (and healthier) alternative to fried doughnuts and are also simple to make gluten- and dairy-free. And the winter squash variation gives the doughnuts a lovely velvety texture.

GLAZE

1 cup (125 g) confectioners' sugar

1 tablespoon almond butter

1 tablespoon plus 2 teaspoons almond milk

Pinch of fine sea salt

DOUGHNUTS

1 cup (120 g) chickpea flour

¼ cup (28 g) oat flour

⅔ cup (96 g) coconut sugar

¼ cup (30 g) arrowroot powder

1 teaspoon baking powder

½ teaspoon baking soda

½ teaspoon fine sea salt

½ teaspoon ground cinnamon

½ teaspoon ground nutmeg

¼ teaspoon ground ginger

2 large eggs

½ cup (120 ml) almond milk

½ cup (128 g) squash puree*

¼ cup (60 ml) coconut oil, melted

1 teaspoon pure vanilla extract

MAPLE WALNUTS

½ cup (535 g) chopped walnuts

1 tablespoon maple syrup

¼ teaspoon coconut oil, melted or very soft

¼ teaspoon coarse sea salt

1 Whisk together the confectioners' sugar, almond butter, milk, and salt until smooth; set aside until ready to use.

2 Preheat oven to 350°F (180°C) and grease a 12-cavity doughnut pan (or two 6-cavity doughnut pans); set aside.

3 In a large bowl, whisk together the flours, coconut sugar, arrowroot, baking powder, baking soda, salt, and spices. Set aside.

4 In another large bowl, whisk together the eggs, milk, squash puree, oil, and vanilla. Pour the wet mix into the dry and mix until thoroughly combined. Transfer the batter to a batter bowl or measuring bowl (this makes pouring batter into the doughnut molds easier), and pour into the doughnut molds, filling each three-quarters of the way. Bake in the oven for 13 to 15 minutes, until a cake tester comes out clean.

5 Allow the doughnuts to cool until ready to handle; then remove from the pan and allow to cool completely, about 1 hour.

6 While the doughnuts are cooling, make the maple walnuts. Preheat oven to 350°F (180°C), and line a baking sheet with parchment paper. In a small bowl, toss together the walnuts, syrup, oil, and coarse salt. Turn out the mixture onto the baking sheet and spread out into an even layer. Bake for 8 to 10 minutes, until roasted and sticky. Remove from the oven and let cool. Once cool, chop the nuts and set aside.

7 Remove the glaze from the refrigerator, whisk if need be, and gently dunk the tops of the doughnuts into the glaze; transfer to a plate or platter. Sprinkle the maple walnuts over top and serve immediately.

8 Doughnuts can be stored at room temperature in an airtight container for up to 2 days.

*Note: For the best results, store-bought, canned squash is best here; homemade squash tends to be more on the watery side.

Spiced Scones with Crushed Cranberries

MAKES: 8 SCONES // **PREP TIME:** 10 MINUTES // **COOK TIME:** 16 TO 18 MINUTES

These scones are more on the lightly sweet, tender side as far as scones go. They're sweetened with just a couple of tablespoons of sugar and are filled with ground ginger and cinnamon to balance out the tartness of the cranberries. The recipe calls for crushing the cranberries in a food processor; this gives the scones beautiful flecks of pink cranberry strewn throughout. These are best served fresh, but can be eaten up to 2 days after baking, and are even better when warmed in the oven for a few minutes.

1 cup (120 g) chickpea flour

½ cup (55 g) sorghum flour, plus extra for dusting

¼ cup (28 g) plus 2 tablespoons oat flour

¼ cup (50 g) cane sugar

2 tablespoons arrowroot powder

1 tablespoon baking powder

1 teaspoon orange zest

1 teaspoon psyllium husk powder

1 teaspoon ground ginger

½ teaspoon ground cinnamon

½ teaspoon sea salt

½ cup (120 ml) coconut milk

¼ cup (60 ml) sunflower oil, plus more for your hands

2 large eggs

½ cup (55 g) cranberries, pulverized in a food processor

❶ Preheat oven to 400°F (200°C).

❷ In a large bowl, whisk together the flours, sugar, arrowroot, baking powder, zest, psyllium husk, spices, and salt. In a separate bowl, whisk together the milk, oil, and 1 egg; mix the wet ingredients into the dry, then fold in the cranberries until just combined.

❸ Line a work surface with parchment paper and dust with sorghum flour; turn the dough out onto the surface, lightly oil your hands, and shape the dough into an 8-inch round with a 1-inch thickness.

❹ Crack the remaining egg in a small dish and whisk; set aside. With a sharp knife, score the dough into eighths (so the scones can be easily broken apart later); gently slip a baking sheet underneath the parchment. Use a pastry brush to gently brush the tops and sides of the scones with egg wash; transfer to the oven and bake for 16 to 18 minutes, until lightly browned.

❺ Let the scones cool completely, then take a sharp knife and break the scones into eight pieces.

Cacao Waffles

MAKES: 10 WAFFLES // **PREP TIME:** 5 MINUTES // **COOK TIME:** 20 TO 25 MINUTES

December is a tough month as far as weather goes. It's the month that goes from fall to winter in one fell swoop, and sometimes chocolate is the only thing that makes the cold and bitter temperatures bearable—at least for me. When I think of chocolate in the morning, a sugar rush comes to mind. However, by using cacao powder instead of baking chocolate these waffles are less decadent and more wholesome. I especially love topping these waffles with pomegranate seeds—their tartness bursts with every bite and tastes delicious with the cocoa flavor.

1 cup (120 g) chickpea flour

½ cup (55 g) sorghum flour

½ cup (40 g) cacao powder

½ cup (72 g) coconut sugar

1½ teaspoons baking powder

1 teaspoon baking soda

½ teaspoon sea salt

1¼ cups (300 ml) almond milk

¼ cup (60 ml) coconut oil, melted

2 large eggs

½ teaspoon pure vanilla extract

Maple syrup

¼ cup (38 g) pomegranate seeds

1 In a large bowl, whisk together the flours, cacao, sugar, baking powder, baking soda, and salt. Set aside.

2 In a separate bowl, whisk together the milk, oil, eggs, and vanilla. Combine the wet ingredients into the dry, and mix thoroughly until combined and no lumps remain.

3 Set the waffle iron on medium-high, and place a baking sheet inside the oven set to 200°F (98°C).

4 Grease the iron with oil, and pour on a scant ¼ cup of batter. Let cook for 2 to 3 minutes, until the edges are crisp; transfer the waffle to the warm baking sheet while you cook the remaining waffles. Repeat the process until no batter remains.

5 Serve warm with maple syrup and pomegranate seeds.

Baby Kale Caesar Salad ⓥ

SERVES: 4 TO 6 // **PREP TIME:** 12 HOURS // **COOK TIME:** 1 HOUR

When I was younger, all I would eat was a Caesar pasta salad from a store near my house. They served it with a buttermilk Caesar dressing that was so good I imagine dunking anything in it would have been delightful. There are countless vegan Caesar salad dressings that come very close to the original, but when I first tasted this vegan iteration of a classic Caesar dressing, I almost couldn't tell the difference. When chickpea flour and water are heated and thickened, it provides the creamy base this dressing depends on and contributes a smooth, velvety consistency that's hard to come by in dairy-free recipes.

¼ cup (33 g) raw cashews, soaked overnight and drained

1 cup (240 ml) water

¼ cup (30 g) chickpea flour

2 tablespoons extra virgin olive oil

2 tablespoons lemon juice

2 teaspoons quality Dijon mustard (preferably Maille)

1 teaspoon apple cider vinegar

2 garlic cloves, roughly chopped

½ teaspoon sea salt

Freshly ground pepper

5 cups (125 g) baby kale

½ cup walnut pieces, plus more for shaving

1 ripe avocado, sliced

2 lemon wedges

❶ Place the cashews in an upright high-speed blender; set aside.

❷ In a small saucepan, whisk together the water and flour. Turn the heat to medium and continue whisking. Whisk for 5 to 6 minutes, until the mixture thickens to about the consistency of a roux or melted cheese. Remove from the heat immediately and carefully add it to the blender.

❸ Add the oil, lemon juice, mustard, vinegar, garlic, salt, and pepper, to taste. Blend on high for 1 minute, stopping and scraping down the sides of the blender. Transfer to a lidded jar or cover with plastic wrap; place in refrigerator for at least 1 hour or up to 3 days. When ready to use, place in a food processor or blender, and blend until smooth and creamy; add water a ½ teaspoon at a time until dressing has reached a fluid consistency.

❹ Place the kale in a large serving bowl, drizzle in about ¼ of the Caesar dressing and walnut pieces, and give it all a good toss. Use a microplane and shave a few of the reserved walnuts. Serve with sliced avocado and a squeeze of lemon juice.

Celery Root Latkes

SERVES: 4 TO 6 // **PREP TIME:** 30 MINUTES // **COOK TIME:** 20 MINUTES

This latke recipe is borrowed from my great-grandmother, who, with my grandfather and my great-aunt, came to America via Ellis Island in the 1920s from Aachen, Germany. Although I never knew her, the few recipes she left with our family have become a tradition to make, especially around the holidays. Each year for Hanukkah, my mom and I would make her famous German potato pancakes, which are very similar to latkes. The recipe was never written down, but was practiced and memorized, and, over the years, I've learned the recipe by heart as well. Celery root (or celeriac), despite its name, is not the root of celery stalks; it's a homely root vegetable with a flavor similar to celery, but it has a smooth nutty taste that only adds to the flavor of a traditional latke.

¼ cup (30 g) chickpea flour

1 small celery root (1 lb/475 g), peeled, greens removed

2 medium Yukon Gold potatoes (1 lb/470 g), peeled

1 medium onion

2 large eggs

2 tablespoons chopped parsley, plus extra for serving

1 teaspoon baking powder

1 teaspoon sea salt

Freshly ground pepper

½ cup sunflower oil

Chickpea Sour Cream (page 152)

1 Heat a skillet over medium heat. Once the pan is hot, add the flour; cook until toasted and golden, stirring every few seconds to avoid scorching, about 6 to 7 minutes. Remove from the heat and place in a bowl to cool.

2 On a box grater using the coarse holes, grate the celery root, potatoes, and onion; place in a large fine-mesh sieve over a bowl and use your hands to press as much liquid out as you can.

3 Add the eggs to a large bowl and whisk; add the vegetable mixture and mix until vegetables are coated. Mix in the toasted flour, parsley, baking powder, salt, and pepper, to taste, until thoroughly combined.

4 Heat ¼ cup of the oil in a large skillet over medium-high heat until the oil is hot and shimmering. In batches, use a spoon to scoop 2 tablespoons' worth of latke mixture into the pan; flatten with the back of your spoon so the latke is about ¼ inch. Cook for 2 to 3 minutes, until golden brown and crisp. Gently turn the latkes over and cook the other side for 1 to 2 minutes. Using a slotted spatula, transfer to a paper towel–lined plate. Repeat the frying process with the remaining oil and latke batter, and use more paper towels to layer each batch. These are best served hot off the stove or warmed in the oven with a helping of chickpea sour cream and chopped parsley.

Roasted Kabocha Squash with Black Rice and Chickpea-Sesame Dressing ⓥ

SERVES: 4 // **PREP TIME:** 20 MINUTES // **COOK TIME:** 30 TO 35 MINUTES

Kabocha squash may be my favorite variety of winter squash. It has a deep green, knobby—but beautiful—exterior, and a rich flavorful flesh that's sweeter than most butternut squash. It's great in soups and stews, but I find that its flavor really comes out when it's roasted in the oven, just to the point where its edges get caramelized and its interior is tender and sweet. I love this dish for so many reasons—for its flavor and textures, but also its wonderfully vibrant colors that are such a difference from the oranges, browns, and reds for which this season is known.

2½ cups (600 ml) water

2 tablespoons chickpea flour

2 tablespoons tahini paste

1 garlic clove, roughly chopped

2 tablespoons extra virgin olive oil

2 teaspoons rice vinegar

1 teaspoon toasted sesame oil

1 teaspoon tamari

½ teaspoon maple syrup

¼ teaspoon fine sea salt

Coarse sea salt

Freshly ground pepper

½ kabocha squash, cut into 1-inch pieces

1 cup (190 g) black rice

1 red onion, cut into 8 wedges with root attached

¼ cup (15 g) chopped cilantro

1 tablespoon toasted sesame seeds

❶ In a small saucepan, whisk together a ½ cup of water and the flour until incorporated and no lumps remain. Turn the heat to medium-low and continue to whisk for 4 to 5 minutes, until mixture thickens. Once it thickens, remove from the heat immediately and pour into a blender. Add the tahini, garlic, 1 tablespoon of olive oil, vinegar, sesame oil, tamari, syrup, fine salt, and pepper, to taste, until smooth. Taste and adjust salt if needed. Cover with plastic wrap and refrigerate until ready to use.

❷ Preheat oven to 400°F (200°C) and line a rimmed baking sheet with parchment paper. Set aside.

❸ In a large bowl, toss the squash and onion with the remaining tablespoon of olive oil, season with a good pinch of coarse salt and a few cracks of pepper. Transfer to the baking sheet and roast for 30 to 35 minutes, until tender and the edges are lightly browned.

❹ While the squash is roasting, cook the rice. Bring 2 cups of water to a boil, add the rice and a pinch of coarse salt. Let the water come back to a boil, cover, and turn the heat to low. Cook for 25 minutes, until the water has evaporated and the rice is tender.

❺ Remove the dressing from the refrigerator and whisk; if dressing is too thick, add water 1 teaspoon at a time until you reach your desired consistency.

❻ Place the rice in a large serving bowl. Add the roasted squash, onion, cilantro, and sesame seeds. Add 3 to 4 tablespoons of dressing and combine as desired.

Matzo Ball Soup

MAKES: 18 MATZO BALLS // **SERVES:** 9 // **PREP TIME:** 3 HOURS // **COOK TIME:** 20 TO 22 MINUTES

This recipe is special, partly for its simplicity, but mostly because of the family memories it holds. Every Jewish holiday in my house was celebrated with a bowl of matzo ball soup, whether the observance called for it or not. Rosh Hashanah: matzo ball soup. Passover: matzo ball soup. Hanukkah: potato latkes and matzo ball soup. It was a go-to we all enjoyed and something that was so tasty and simple. While most (if not all) store-bought matzo ball soup contains gluten, this gluten-free version tastes exactly like the original. These matzo balls are fluffy and dense in just the right places, but are a bit more delicate, which is why I advise to cook them in batches. I like to serve with a side of roasted carrots.

1½ cups (180 g) chickpea flour

2 teaspoons baking powder

1 teaspoon sea salt

Freshly ground pepper

3 large eggs

3 tablespoons extra virgin olive oil

6 cups (1,440 ml) vegetable broth

2 tablespoons chopped dill

❶ In a bowl, whisk together the flour, baking powder, salt, and pepper, to taste. In a separate bowl, whisk together the eggs and oil until just combined. Make a hole in the center of the flour mixture and add the egg mix. Fold together with a rubber spatula until thoroughly incorporated; the batter will be very thick and sticky. Cover with plastic wrap and refrigerate for 3 hours.

❷ Fill a large lidded pot three-quarters full with water and bring to a simmer. Place the broth in another large pot and bring to a simmer, cover, and turn the heat to low.

❸ While the water is heating, remove the matzo ball batter from the refrigerator; take about 2 teaspoons' worth of batter (roughly 20 to 22 grams) and, with wet hands, roll the dough between your palms to make balls. Bring the simmering water to a boil. Gently drop half the matzo balls into the water; when the balls rise to the surface, turn the heat down to a simmer and cover the pot. Cook for 20 to 22 minutes, until the matzo balls are cooked through and the centers are light. If the center is hard and dark, cook for another 3 to 5 minutes, until the center is cooked and light. Transfer to the warmed broth, and repeat with the remaining matzo balls.

❹ Bring the vegetable broth and matzo balls to a simmer. Serve one to two matzo balls per serving; garnish with dill.

Jammy Almond Thumbprint Cookies

MAKES: 22 COOKIES // **PREP TIME:** 15 MINUTES // **COOK TIME:** 8 TO 10 MINUTES

These are an adaptation of a favorite holiday cookie my mother and I would make—minus the pounds of butter. The cookie dough is slightly sweet and gently flavored by the coconut oil and almond extract. The dough is then rolled through chopped almonds, baked, and topped with jam or preserves of your choosing. These cookies are best stored at room temperature covered loosely with a piece of parchment paper for up to 2 days.

1 cup (100 g) almond flour

1 cup (120 g) chickpea flour

¼ teaspoon baking soda

¼ teaspoon sea salt

¼ cup (60 ml) coconut oil, melted

2 tablespoons maple syrup

1 large egg, plus the white from 1 large egg

⅛ teaspoon almond extract

½ cup (35 g) slivered almonds, roughly chopped

Blackberry jam or preserves (or jam of choice)

① Preheat oven to 350°F (180°C), and line two cookie sheets with parchment paper; set aside.

② In a large bowl, whisk together the flours, baking soda, and salt. In a separate bowl, whisk together the oil, syrup, 1 whole egg, and almond extract. Using a spatula, mix the wet ingredients into the dry, folding the dough until thoroughly combined.

③ Place the egg white into a small bowl, whisk, and set aside. Place the chopped slivered almonds in a separate bowl and set aside.

④ Scoop the dough out and roll into balls the size of a quarter, dip the balls into the egg whites, then gently press them into the almonds, and place on the cookie sheets. Use your palm to flatten the cookies to a ¼-inch thickness.

⑤ Bake for 8 to 10 minutes, until lightly golden. Remove from the oven and immediately use the back of a small spoon to make a divot in the top of each cookie and let cool.

⑥ Once the cookies are cool, spoon about ¼ teaspoon of jam into each divot.

Parsnip-Pear Bundt Cake

MAKES: 1 EIGHT-INCH ROUND BUNDT CAKE // **SERVES:** 8 TO 10 // **PREP TIME:** 25 MINUTES
COOK TIME: 50 TO 60 MINUTES

I love the opportunity to mix vegetables and fruit together in a savory or sweet dish. At first thought, you would not think of parsnips as a complement to cake. Parsnips, much like carrots in flavor, shape, and size, are a bit sweeter and have a peppery smell when raw. But when shredded and baked into a cake they offer a wonderful balance to a sweet cake as well as a lovely texture. This Bundt cake is a tried-and-true cake recipe that first started out as a fruitcake but has, over time, come to be more of a humble spice cake that celebrates the season's sweet and savory produce.

1 cup (120 g) chickpea flour

½ cup (50 g) almond flour

½ cup (70 g) brown rice flour

¼ cup (30 g) arrowroot powder

2 teaspoons baking powder

1 teaspoon ground ginger

1 teaspoon ground nutmeg

½ teaspoon baking soda

½ teaspoon ground cinnamon

¼ teaspoon sea salt

1 cup (144 g) coconut sugar

½ cup (120 ml) sunflower oil

3 large eggs

1 cup (250 g) applesauce

2 teaspoons pure vanilla extract

1 cup (85 g) grated parsnips

1 ripe but firm pear,
cut into ¼-inch chunks

½ cup (50 g) chopped pecans

Confectioners' sugar, for dusting

❶ Preheat oven to 350°F (180°C) and grease an 8-inch Bundt pan. Set aside.

❷ In a large bowl, whisk together the flours, arrowroot, baking powder, ginger, nutmeg, baking soda, cinnamon, and salt. Set aside.

❸ Using the whisk attachment on an electric mixer, whisk together the sugar and oil, until wet and sandy. Whisk the eggs in one at a time, then whisk in the applesauce and vanilla until thoroughly combined. Fold in the parsnips, pear, and pecans.

❹ A little at a time, mix the dry ingredients into the wet, until thoroughly combined. Evenly distribute the batter into the prepared Bundt pan and bake for 50 to 60 minutes, until a cake tester inserted into the middle comes out clean.

❺ Let the cake cool completely before removing from the pan. Just before serving, dust the top of the cake with confectioners' sugar.

Acknowledgments

Much gratitude is due to the following people:

To my dearest husband, Frank, who has not only encouraged me, held my hand, and listened to my worries endlessly, but also without whom this path would not have been possible. Thank you for taste-testing recipes and making countless trips to the grocery store, and, most important, thank you for being the calm in the storm. I love you beyond measure.

To my loving and supportive parents, who taught me to dream big and dream beyond the rainbow. Your insistence on following my heart has led me to find what I'm most passionate about.

Thank you, Brad, for being the best big brother and best friend I know. Your pep talks, love, and reassurance have always meant everything to me.

To my Love family, thank you for the encouragement and love throughout this time and for your support.

To my incredible agent, Judy Linden, without whom this book would have never happened. Thank you for guiding me through a process I was completely blind to, for your constant cheerleading, and, most important, your friendship.

To my editor, Allie Bochicchio, for allowing me to create this book and make it mine. Thank you to the entire Experiment team—especially Matthew Lore, Dan O'Connor, Sarah Smith, Sarah Schneider, Jennifer Hergenroeder, Karen Giangreco, Vivienne Woodward, and Batya Rosenblum—for believing in my vision for this book and supporting me along the way.

To all the recipe testers who gave such invaluable feedback; big thanks especially to Sara Cornelius, Edlyn D'Souza, Erica Kwee, Ashley McLaughlin, Grace Rusch, and Nik Sharma. Thank you to Candice Uyloan and Sarah Smith for your guidance and help throughout the various stages of this journey.

Last, but certainly not least, thank you to the readers of *Dolly and Oatmeal* who have always been so kind and generous with their comments and questions; without you this book would have never come to fruition.

Index

Note: Page references in *italics* indicate photographs.

About the Author

LINDSEY S. LOVE
is a food stylist, food photographer,
recipe developer, and blogger
living in Brooklyn, New York,
with her husband and dog. She is
the creator of the blog *Dolly and
Oatmeal*, which has been a finalist
for *Saveur* magazine's Food Blog
Awards numerous times—for
Best Original Recipes and, most
recently, for Best Special Interest
Blog. Her work has been featured
in *Thoughtfully* magazine, *Food52*,
the *Huffington Post*, People.com,
Buzzfeed, *Epicurious*, *InStyle*,
and *Saveur*.